Farewell to the Leftist Working Class

Farewell to the Leftist Working Class

Dick Houtman
Peter Achterberg
Anton Derks

TRANSACTION PUBLISHERS
NEW BRUNSWICK (U.S.A.) AND LONDON (U.K.)

Copyright © 2008 by Transaction Publishers, New Brunswick, New Jersey.

All rights reserved under International and Pan-American Copyright Conventions. No part of this book may be reproduced or transmitted in any form or by any means, electronic or mechanical, including photocopy, recording, or any information storage and retrieval system, without prior permission in writing from the publisher. All inquiries should be addressed to Transaction Publishers, Rutgers—The State University of New Jersey, 35 Berrue Circle, Piscataway, New Jersey 08854-8042. www.transactionpub.com

This book is printed on acid-free paper that meets the American National Standard for Permanence of Paper for Printed Library Materials.

Library of Congress Catalog Number: 2007033682
ISBN: 978-1-4128-0693-0
Printed in the United States of America

Library of Congress Cataloging-in-Publication Data

Houtman, Dick.
  Farewell to the leftist working class / Dick Houtman, Peter Achterberg, and Anton Derks.
  Includes bibliographical references and index.
  ISBN 978-1-4128-0693-0 (acid-free paper)
    1. Working class—Political activity. 2. Right and left (Political science) I. Achterberg, Peter. II. Derks, Anton. III. Title.

HD6487.5.H68 2008
323'.04208623—dc22   2007033682

Contents

Preface		vii
1.	The Specter of the Rightist Working Class	1
2.	What Drives "Unnatural" Voting? A Cultural Explanation for Voting Behavior	15
3.	A Cross-Pressured Working Class? Class Voting, Cultural Voting, and Issue Salience	37
4.	The End of Left and Right? The Transformation of Political Culture (1945-1998)	55
5.	A Decline of Class Voting? Class Voting and Cultural Voting in the Postwar Era (1956-1990) (with Jeroen van der Waal)	71
6.	The Working Class and the Welfare State: Judgments on the Rights and Obligations of the Unemployed	91
7.	Is Working-Class Economic Egalitarianism Really that Politically Progressive? Economic Populism, Egalitarianism, and Political Progressiveness	105
8.	Conclusion Class Is Not Dead—It Has Been Buried Alive	119

Appendix 1: Measurement of Four Types of Issue Salience   125

Appendix 2: Secondary Data Sources   127

References   129

About the Authors   141

Index   143

Preface

This book is the result of our research efforts into problems of class and politics, conducted since two of us published earlier books on the subject: *Individualisme zonder verhaal* (Individualism without a Cause), Anton Derks (2000), and *Class and Politics in Contemporary Social Science*, Dick Houtman (2003). Dick Houtman has since 2002 collaborated with the third musketeer, Peter Achterberg, who has completed his Ph.D. thesis, *Considering Cultural Conflict* (2006), in the meantime under his supervision.

Although we are glad to assume joint responsibility for this book, we want to point out to the reader that all draft chapters have been edited—in some instances quite drastically—by this book's first author. Apart from this final editing, Peter Achterberg is responsible for Chapter 4, Dick Houtman for Chapter 6, and Anton Derks for Chapter 7. Chapters 2 and 3 are co-productions by Peter Achterberg and Dick Houtman, who have collaborated with Jeroen van der Waal in writing Chapter 5. Jeroen is a Ph.D. student at Erasmus University's Sociology Department and Chapter 5 is based on the MA thesis he completed in 2005, supervised by Peter Achterberg and Dick Houtman. The subtitle of the concluding chapter, *Class Is Not Dead—It Has Been Buried Alive*, was also thought up by Jeroen. It nicely summarizes the main theoretical point that we want to make in this book. Finally, Chapters 1 and 8 were written by Dick Houtman, drawing partially on materials supplied by Peter Achterberg and Anton Derks, of course.

We want to thank Transaction's Irving Louis Horowitz—not only for his interest in this book project, but also for his patience, because its completion has taken more time than we envisaged at the start. Thanks are also due to Andrew McIntosh for his careful editing of the manuscript. Finally, we want to acknowledge Mylène Malipaard and Roy Kemmers, both sociology students at Erasmus University, for their invaluable research assistance. Mylène did a great job in taking care of the tables and figures and the list of literature references, and Roy accurately and efficiently tracked down a number of relevant literature sources.

Dick Houtman, Peter Achterberg, and Anton Derks
Rotterdam/Brussels
December 2006

1

The Specter of the Rightist Working Class

Introduction

A specter is haunting the long-standing class theory of politics—the specter of the rightist working class. Although large parts of the social-scientific community still consider it the natural support base for leftist political agendas, the working class has increasingly come to support rightist parties, even the populist ones that harshly critique the welfare state, the institutional flagship of the left. Hardly surprising, then, today's social-scientific literature is rife with publications that proclaim a dramatic decline of the political significance of class since World War II. Especially Clark and Lipset's (1991) article "Are Social Classes Dying?" sparked a lively debate, which has yielded books such as *The Death of Class* (Pakulski and Waters 1996), *The End of Class Politics?* (Evans 1999a), and *The Breakdown of Class Politics* (Clark and Lipset 2001, see Clark 2001a for an overview of this debate).

The outcome of this "death of class debate" so far seems to be that although it would certainly be too far-fetched to announce class "dead," it indeed affects political life in contemporary western countries to a lesser extent than it used to do a few decades ago (e.g., Evans et al. 1999, Weakliem and Heath 1999a, 1999b, see however Evans 2000). "With respect to politics, social classes are certainly not dead, but the rumours of their imminent death are not all that exaggerated," as Nieuwbeerta (2001: 132) succinctly summarizes the newly grown intellectual consensus (see also Brooks et al. 2006). Naturally, this gradual disappearance of the leftist working class also raises doubts about the contemporary validity of the class theory of politics, which holds that people follow their class-based economic interests when acting politically.

Now these are certainly not the first indications that something is wrong with the class theory of politics. Social and political reality already refused to conform to theoretically informed predictions in the mid-19th century, when Marx wrote confidently that "Universal Suffrage is the equivalent of political power for the working class of England, where the proletariat forms the large majority of the population. ... Its inevitable result, here, is the political supremacy of the working class" (1963 [1852]: 204-7). When a few years later, in 1867, members of the British parliament prepared the Second Reform Bill, which would give the vote to a large part of the working class, they were indeed afraid this would cause them to lose power to the left. Their anxiety proved completely misplaced, however: many workers failed to vote for the left and the right remained in power (McKenzie and Silver 1968).

What is wrong, then, with the class theory of politics? Why does the working class increasingly vote for rightist parties, even the populist ones that have since the 1980s unleashed an attack on the welfare state in many European countries? Indeed, why is working-class support for the welfare state so remarkably limited today? These are questions that we address in this book. In this opening chapter, we first explain why the class theory of politics itself cannot satisfactorily account for these rightist tendencies among the working class and then proceed to outline a more promising alternative explanation. We complete this introductory chapter with a brief discussion of the data that will be analyzed in the chapters that follow and a brief outline of the rest of the book.

Declining Class Politics?

Increased Rightist Voting by the Working Class

The notion of politics as driven by class-based economic interests underlies not only Marx's classical work about the dynamics of capitalist society (Marx and Engels 1948 [1848], Marx 1967 [1867]), but also the influential and virtually uncontested conception of voting as an expression of a "democratic class struggle" (Lipset and Rokkan 1967, Lipset 1981). Given this long-standing theoretical tradition, it is not without significance that the familiar alignment of the working class with the left has declined considerably in most Western countries since World War II. This has most convincingly been demonstrated by Nieuwbeerta's (1995, 1996) large-scale study of class voting in more than a dozen western countries since World War II, the most relevant findings of which have been reprinted in *The End of Class Politics?* (Evans 1999a) and *The Breakdown of Class Politics* (Clark and Lipset 2001).[1]

To be fair to the class theory of politics, this gradual erosion of the working-class alignment with leftist parties does not necessarily mean that it is slowly but surely becoming obsolete. We need to distinguish sharply, after all, between the theoretically naïve claim that class divisions always and everywhere structure political life and a mature class theory that is able to predict the conditions under which class divisions actually do so. What, for instance, if the economic position of the working class improves to such an extent that it no longer has a class-based interest in supporting leftist political agendas? What if clear-cut class boundaries give way to gradual status and income hierarchies, blurring income differences between classes and increasing chances for upward mobility for those born in working-class families? Wouldn't that represent an "indispensable ... step on the road to full-fledged middle class status" for the working class (Mayer, quoted by MacKenzie 1967:29)? What, in short, if the thesis of *embourgeoisement* holds (Kerr et al. 1960, Zweig 1961), according to which rising levels of affluence blur the boundaries between working class and middle class, leading the former to adopt the latter's values and lifestyle?

This thesis has influentially been critiqued in the late 1960s, when Goldthorpe et al. (1969) demonstrated that increased working-class affluence did not lead to *embourgeoisement* in the United Kingdom. This not only means that class boundaries remained socially and politically salient there and then, however, but also that something is seriously wrong with the class theory of politics. The notion that impoverishment (*Verelendung*) strengthens class consciousness, while increasing affluence undermines it (*embourgeoisement*) is a mainstay of this theory, after all. The notion of *Verelendung* features prominently in the *Manifesto of the Communist Party* (Marx and Engels 1948 [1848]), while Lenin adopted that of *embourgeoisement* when he argued that colonial exploitation produced a high living standard in 19th-century Britain that hampered class consciousness, approvingly quoting from letters in which Friedrich Engels makes the same argument. In a letter to Karl Kautsky, dated September 12, 1882, for instance, Engels observed that "[T]he workers gaily share the feast of England's monopoly of the world market and the colonies"; and in a letter to Karl Marx, dated October 7, 1858, he observed that "The English proletariat is actually becoming more and more bourgeois, so that this most bourgeois of all nations is apparently aiming ultimately at the possession of a bourgeois aristocracy and a bourgeois proletariat *alongside* the bourgeoisie" (both letters quoted in Lenin 1968 [1916]:246).

As a vital element of the class theory of politics, in short, the thesis of *embourgeoisement* makes predictions about the circumstances under which class divisions are more or less socially and politically salient. This means that in itself the gradual erosion of the familiar pattern of a leftist-voting working class and a rightist-voting middle class since World War II does not contradict the class theory of politics. Precisely against this background, however, a set of less widely published findings from Nieuwbeerta's aforementioned study (1995) raises far more annoying questions about its validity. As it happens, trying to "(remain) as close as possible within the class perspective" (1995:201), Nieuwbeerta tests a set of hypotheses derived from the thesis of *embourgeoisement*, aimed at predicting the strength of the relationship between class and voting in the various countries and periods. These hypotheses pertain to socio-economic context variables such as the magnitude of the income differences, the living standard, the percentage of intergenerational mobility, and the number of manual workers as a percentage of the population. Remarkable as it may seem, these hypotheses are refuted almost without exception (Ibid.: 57-77).

As we see it, this failure of the class theory of politics to even remotely accurately predict the circumstances under which class divisions are politically salient should far more disturb its advocates than the gradual disappearance of the leftist-voting working class itself. It leads us to the first question that we will address in this book: how to explain increasingly rightist voting by the working class if the class theory of politics itself is incapable of doing so?

Limited Working-Class Support for the Welfare State

The class theory of politics also faces difficulties in explaining the extremely limited working-class support for the welfare state today. Following the logic of the class theory of politics, after all, the welfare state is a working-class interest *par excellence*, because one of its principal aims is the decommodification of labor by weakening the link between work and income (Marshall 1965, Esping-Andersen 1990). Why, then, does the working class hardly support the welfare state more ardently than society's more privileged classes (Van Oorschot 1998: 72)?

Like increased rightist voting by the working class, the absence of clear working-class support for the welfare state can in principle also be explained from the logic of the class theory of politics itself—more specifically, again, from the thesis of *embourgeoisement*. The latter leads us to expect, after all, that an improvement of the economic position of the working class wipes out not only its loyalty to leftist political parties, but also the economic egalitarianism on which this loyalty is based. The problem with this class-theory based explanation, however, is that apart from the absence of clear working-class support for the welfare state there are no other signs of a disappearance of working-class economic egalitarianism. More than that: there are many studies that demonstrate that the working class still sets itself apart from society's more privileged classes by means of higher levels of economic egalitarianism (e.g., Marshall et al. 1988: 179-183, Middendorp 1991, Scheepers et al. 1992, Weakliem and Heath 1994, Elchardus 1996, De Witte and Billiet 1999, Edlund 1999, Svallfors 1999, Houtman 2003). How to explain the absence of clear working-class support for the welfare state, then, if these other signs of *embourgeoisement* are non-existent? This is the second question that we will address in this book.

Increasing Cultural Politics?

A New Political Culture?

Our point of departure in explaining increasing rightist tendencies among the working class is the so-called "theory of the new political culture," according to which cultural issues have increasingly come to the fore since the 1960s (e.g., Dalton et al. 1984, Rempel and Clark 1997, Clark 1998, 2001b, Hechter 2004, Weakliem 2001). This theory is particularly related to the name of Ronald Inglehart. Ever since the publication of his path-breaking book, *The Silent Revolution* (1977), he has maintained that due to increasing affluence, "postmaterialist" values, pertaining to the primacy of individual liberty and self-attainment, have become substantially more widespread in Western countries (1990, 1997). Even though it is often credited for this, however, Inglehart's work on the political ramifications of a cultural shift towards postmaterialist values cannot carry the weight of the claim that the emergence of a new political culture has caused a decline of class politics.

Although it is uncontested that a "postmaterialist" value orientation has become more widespread in western countries during the last few decades, it is not clear what this says about changes in the political culture. As we will argue in more detail in Chapter 3, Inglehart's "postmaterialism" index collapses authoritarianism/libertarianism with the type of issues considered most salient and because of this, it is quite unclear what the increased spread of postmaterialism means. This is especially so, because Inglehart's index does not allow for the possibility that left-libertarian and right-authoritarian cultural issues have both become more salient.[2] It rules out "right-authoritarian postmaterialism" by definition, thus enabling increased right-authoritarian issue salience to remain undetected by flying under the radar of the postmaterialism index.

This neglect of the possibility of "right-authoritarian postmaterialism" is of course quite problematical, given that new rightist-populist parties, emphasizing cultural issues more than anything else—yet doing so from a right-authoritarian rather than a left-libertarian angle—have been electorally successful all over Europe since the 1980s (Ignazi 1992, 2003, Veugelers 2000). Examples are the FPÖ in Austria, the Schweizerische Volkspartei (SVP) in Switzerland, the Progress Party (FrP) and the Danish People's Party (DF) in Denmark, the Progress Party (FrP) in Norway, the Vlaams Blok (renamed to Vlaams Belang in 2004) in Flanders, Belgium, the Republikäner in Germany, the Front National in France, and the Lijst Pim Fortuyn (LPF) in the Netherlands. It is not clear at all, in short, what the increased spread of "postmaterialism" in western countries during the last few decades tells us about changes in the political culture.

Declining Class Voting or Increasing Cultural Voting?

Even if cultural issues have become more salient since World War II and even if it is true that "Postmaterialists come from middle-class backgrounds" and that "middle-class Postmaterialists move left ... and working-class materialists move to the right," it still remains to be seen whether "this is conducive to a decline in class voting," as Inglehart (1997: 254) suggests. As we see it, increasing cultural issue salience is likely to leave class voting intact, while nevertheless eroding the familiar alignment of the working class with the left. As it happens, we expect increasing cultural issue salience to strengthen what we will call cross-cutting "cultural voting" rather than to undermine "class voting." The necessity to distinguish between these two types of voting is informed by two sets of research findings (see also Houtman 2003).

The first set of findings pertains to the existence of two political value domains in western democracies, which are by and large independent of one another. The first domain, referred to as "economic egalitarianism/ conservatism" in this book, pertains to the degree to which one favors either laissez-faire liberalism or economic redistribution by the state. The second domain, referred to as "authoritarianism/libertarianism" in this book, pertains to the degree to which one favors either protection of individual liberty or maintenance of social order and hence includes Inglehart's (1977, 1990, 1997) notion of postmaterialism, too. Already hinted at by Lipset in the 1950s (1959), the virtual absence of a relationship between authoritarianism/libertarianism and economic egalitarianism/conservatism has been found ever since among the mass publics of Western countries (e.g., Mitchell 1966, Kelly and Chambliss 1966, O'Kane 1970, Felling and Peters 1986, De Witte 1990, Fleishman 1988, Middendorp 1991, Scheepers et al. 1992, Olson and Carroll 1992, Heath et al. 1994, Evans et al. 1996, Houtman 2003). This means that among the public at large, one cannot predict without additional information, for instance, whether someone is for or against the death penalty if one knows his or her stance towards income redistribution (and *vice versa*, of course).

The second relevant set of research findings, to be discussed in some more detail in Chapter 2, pertains to the explanation of both types of values. Like the independence of these two types of values, it has been found over and over again since World War II that authoritarianism does not emerge from a low income, but rather from a low level of education. The latter relationship has nevertheless often been interpreted as indicating that authoritarianism, just like economic egalitarianism, emerges from a weak economic position. Likewise, the well-known positive relationship between education and postmaterialism has been interpreted by Inglehart (1977, 1990) as supporting his theory that growing up under conditions of affluence produces a long-lasting commitment to individual liberty and self-attainment. These "Marxist lite" interpretations of the relationship between education and authoritarianism/libertarianism, one of us has demonstrated elsewhere, are not supported by the available evidence, because in this case education operates as an indicator for the amount of cultural capital one has at one's disposal (Houtman 2003).

These two sets of research findings call for a distinction between class voting and cultural voting. Class voting can be conceptualized as voting for a leftist party on the grounds of economically egalitarian political values generated by a weak class position (or, reversely, voting for a rightist political party on the grounds of economically conservative political values generated by a strong class position). Class voting as such needs to be distinguished from cultural voting, which is not driven by class-based economic interests, but rather by cultural capital and related authoritarianism/libertarianism. Cultural voting, then, is voting for a leftist political party on the grounds of libertarian political values generated by ample cultural capital (or, reversely, voting for a rightist political party on the grounds of authoritarian political values generated by limited cultural capital).

**Figure 1.1
Cultural Voting Distinguished from Class Voting**

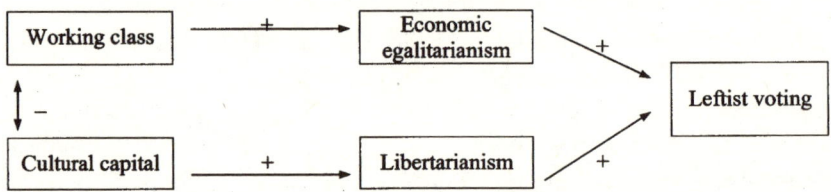

Because cultural capital is, of course, strongly and positively related to class in an economic sense (Bourdieu 1984), yet affects the vote reversely (Figure 1.1), a bivariate relationship between class position and voting behavior tells us basically nothing about the occurrence of class voting. This is quite an important insight, because ever since Alford's (1967) pioneering work in this area in the 1960s, such a bivariate relationship has been taken to indicate precisely this.

Beyond the Alford Index

Alford proposed to measure class voting "by subtracting the percentage of persons in nonmanual occupations voting for 'Left' parties from the percentage of manual workers voting for such parties" (1967: 80). Hence, the more workers vote for leftist parties and the fewer non-workers do so, the higher the level of class voting. This "Alford index," as it soon came to be called, has become an intellectual routine in political sociology since. Its almost universal acceptance is underscored by the circumstance that even the most vocal critics of Clark and Lipset's influential article (1991) accepted the notion that the bivariate relationship between class and voting indicates the level of class voting, even though they argued for the need to develop more statistically advanced varieties (Hout et al. 1993). Because these statistically more advanced varieties are however basically identical from a theoretical point of view, it is hardly surprising that Nieuwbeerta's research points out that they produce identical findings, too: "The main finding is that the various measures of class voting (yield) the same conclusions with respect to the ranking of the countries according to their levels of class voting and according to the speed of declines in class voting" (1996: 370). Besides in Nieuwbeerta's large-scale study of class voting since World War II (1995, 1996, 2001, Nieuwbeerta and De Graaf 1999), Alford-index-based indices of class voting have also been used by a variety of researchers who have contributed chapters to the two key volumes about the class and politics debate, i.e., *The End of Class Politics?* (Evans 1999a) and *The Breakdown of Class Politics* (Clark and Lipset 2001).

As bizarre as it may seem, however, the estimation of levels of class voting by means of Alford indices, basically the standard procedure in this field of research since the 1960s, precludes conclusions about the actual development of class voting. The Alford index does after all not capture the level of class voting, but rather the net balance of class voting and cultural voting—the extent to which class voting is stronger than reversed cultural voting. This raises the question whether the decline of the familiar pattern of a leftist-voting working class and a rightist-voting middle class really indicates a decline of class voting, as it has always been interpreted. Although this may be the case, another possibility is that class voting has not become weaker, but cultural voting stronger. It is even possible that class voting has actually become stronger, while cultural voting has increased even more, thus also producing a decline of the Alford index.

Our distinction between class voting and cultural voting, in short, points out that the declining alignment of the working class with the left does not necessarily indicate a decline of class voting. It as such suggests an explanation for why the class theory of politics has proven incapable of explaining this trend, as demonstrated by Nieuwbeerta's study: because it may not so much indicate a decline of class voting, caused by a declining salience of class issues, as the thesis of *embourgeoisement* would lead us to expect, but rather an increase of cultural voting, caused by the emergence of a new political culture in which cultural issues have become more salient. We study the validity of this alternative theory in Chapters 2 through 5 of this book.

The New Political Culture and the Welfare State

The economic recession that started during the first half of the 1970s created a budgetary crisis that discouraged further expansion of social expenditures (Pierson 1994) and encouraged retrenchment (Korpi and Palme 2003). Although the much-discussed "crisis of the welfare state" that followed was initially seen as first and foremost of a fiscal and budgetary nature, it increasingly came to be seen as a cultural or moral crisis from the 1980s onwards. As a consequence, moral notions of deservingness increasingly came to the fore, casting the welfare state as providing for "welfare scroungers" who exploit hard-working taxpayers (e.g., Gilder 1981, Murray 1984, Mead 1986).

This new cultural discourse about the welfare state, that indeed suggests the emergence of a new political culture in which cultural issues have become more salient, is especially carried by the new rightist-populist parties that have emerged all over Europe since the 1980s. Basically reinventing and remodeling Saint-Simon's (1760-1825) narrative of the parasitic class, used at the time to legitimate newly emerging industrialism, these parties now attack the welfare state (Papadopoulos 2001). While Saint-Simon cast clergy and nobility as parasitic classes, so as to situate both workers and entrepreneurs at the productive and hence "deserving" side of the moral equation, Marx later on drove a wedge between these two industrial classes, casting capitalist entrepreneurs as the exploiting parasitic class (Houtman 2003: 3-6). Today's new rightist-populist remodeling of this narrative resembles its archetypical Saint-Simonian version in that it re-unites working class and entrepreneurs on the "deserving" side of the moral equation. It differs from the latter in that it identifies "welfare scroungers"—typically considered to be immigrants—rather than clergy and nobility as the major parasitic class that exploits the hard-working common man.[3]

The new rightist-populist parties advocate a blunt "welfare chauvinism," which is aimed at restricting entitlements to social security to a deserving ethnically defined in-group (Kitschelt 1995, Mudde 2000). And indeed, if cultural issues are salient, working-class authoritarianism is likely to create a strong desire to restrict entitlements to a deserving in-group of law-abiding citizens—a desire that inevitably detracts substantially from any support for the welfare state that emerges from working-class economic egalitarianism. Drawing sharp symbolic boundaries between itself and the undeserving unemployed enables the working class to situate itself firmly on the "good" and "deserving" side of the moral equation by embracing an authoritarian discourse which features discipline, dignity, hard work and straightforwardness as the central values (Lamont 2000). It is indeed quite telling that the tendency to set oneself apart from "undeserving" welfare beneficiaries who "abuse social security" is not least found among those on welfare themselves (Kochuyt and Derks 2003).

In a political climate in which the welfare state is conceived as a moral rather than an economic problem, in short, the working class easily turns its back against it. Limited working-class support for the welfare state may thus result not so much from limited economic egalitarianism, as the thesis of *embourgeoisement* would lead us to expect, but rather from a high level of authoritarianism. This would mean that the same authoritarianism that presumably drives working-class voting for rightist parties also detracts from support for the welfare state that is produced by working-class economic egalitarianism. We study the validity of this theory in Chapters 6 and 7 of this book.

Data

Data from a wide range of Western countries are analyzed in this book. We obviously use survey data from our home countries, the Netherlands and Dutch-speaking Flanders (Belgium). Dick Houtman collected the Dutch data used in chapters 2 and 6 through the nationally representative panel of Centerdata (University of Tilburg, The Netherlands) in 1997 (see for a more detailed description: Houtman 2003).[4] With the exception of these Dutch survey data, we have collected none of the data used in this book ourselves. Besides survey data that are representative for the Flemish population (Chapter 7), we use American survey data covering the period 1960-2000 (Chapter 3), data on the contents of political party manifestos in twenty Western countries since World War II (Chapter 4), a compilation of survey data from fifteen Western countries since World War II (Chapter 5), and more recent data from the *European Social Survey* (2002) from six western countries (Chapter 7). The Dutch data of the *European Social Survey* are also analyzed in Chapter 2, besides the data that have been collected by this book's first author and that have already been mentioned above. The reader is referred to Appendix 3 for an overview of these secondary data sources.

Design of the Book

Because the long-standing class theory of politics assumes that it is only "natural" for the working class to vote for leftist parties, we start in Chapter 2 with an analysis of why workers would vote for parties that contradict their class-based interests. Critically elaborating on Lipset's work on working-class authoritarianism and Inglehart's on postmaterialism, we demonstrate that the class theory of politics cannot explain such "unnatural" voting. Instead, working-class "unnatural" voting proves to stem from a high level of authoritarianism that is rooted in limited cultural capital, not in a weak economic position. "Natural" voting by the working class can be explained by the class theory of politics, however; its weak economic position engenders economic egalitarianism that drives leftist voting.

Whether and why cross-cutting cultural voting has become more widespread is the question we start to address in Chapter 3. We show that cultural issues have become more salient in the United States during the period 1960-2000, but that this has not gone at the cost of the salience of class issues. Next, we study the consequences of issue salience for the occurrence of class voting and cultural voting. Class voting proves immune to whether or not class issues are salient, while cultural voting is stronger if cultural ones are salient.

In Chapter 4 we then conduct a content analysis of party manifestos from twenty countries since World War II to study whether these reflect the same trends in issue salience as found among the American public since 1960. We find that cultural issues of individual liberty and social order have indeed become more salient and that party polarization with respect to those issues has increased. Although polarization with respect to class-related economic issues has declined somewhat, this type of issues has nevertheless remained as salient as ever. In short, we have been witnessing a radical transformation of left-right polarization since World War II.

Because the findings so far raise doubt about whether the erosion of the familiar pattern of a leftist-voting working class and a rightist-voting middle class since World War II really indicates a decline of class voting, we test the validity of this widely accepted interpretation in Chapter 5. Our re-analysis of Nieuwbeerta's extremely large dataset—covering developments in fifteen Western countries since the 1950s—demonstrates that we are indeed not dealing with a decline of class voting, but rather with an increase of cross-cutting cultural voting.

Chapters 6 and 7 then address working-class support for the welfare state and solidarity with the unemployed. Chapter 6 demonstrates that, although the weak economic position of the working class certainly engenders solidarity with the unemployed, this is washed out by its cultural-capital-based authoritarianism that leads it to apply strict criteria of deservingness. Chapter 7 then demonstrates that in the new political culture working-class (leftist) economic egalitarianism is easily combined with (rightist) aversion to the welfare state. Hardly surprising, then, working-class economic egalitarianism proves to remain strongly particularistic, exclusionary, and self-serving: although obviously less widespread among the middle class, economic egalitarianism is more solidly embedded in a universalistic and inclusionary progressive political ideology there.

Finally, in Chapter 8, we elaborate on the theoretical implications of our research findings. We argue that they point out that we have not so much been witnessing a decline of class politics since World War II, but rather a dramatic increase of cultural politics. With the benefit of hindsight, then, the specter of the rightist working class was merely the by-product of the virtual theoretical monopoly of the class theory of politics in political sociology. Dispelling it requires nothing more than a removal of these theoretical blinders by giving an additional cultural theory of politics its due.

Notes

1. See De Graaf et al. (2001), Dalton (1988), Franklin (1982, 1985), Rose and McAllister (1986), Heath et al. (1996) for more evidence that the relationship between class and voting behavior has declined.
2. Although Inglehart's index obviously allows for the possibility of a "mixed" materialist/postmaterialist position, it fails to acknowledge that the salience of class issues cannot be inferred from that of cultural issues (and *vice versa*). These two types of issues do not exhaust the full range of issue types, after all, and hence should not be treated as limitative and mutually exclusive. It is perfectly possible for cultural issues to become more salient without class issues becoming less so.
3. The new parasitic class as constructed by new-rightist populists also consists of political and bureaucratic elites, as we will explain in Chapter 7.
4. Analyses reported in Chapters 2 and 5 of this book are restricted to panel members who are older than 18 years and working more than 20 hours per week.

2

What Drives "Unnatural" Voting? A Cultural Explanation for Voting Behavior

Introduction

The familiar pattern of a leftist-voting working class and a rightist-voting middle class has declined strongly since World War II, but the class theory of politics is strikingly impotent in explaining why. Hypotheses about the periods and countries in which class distinctions are expected to be most politically salient, pertaining to socio-economic context variables such as the size of income differences, the living standard, the percentage of intergenerational class mobility, trade union density, the relative size of the working class, etc., are rejected almost without exception (Nieuwbeerta 1995, Nieuwbeerta and Ultee 1999).

Now, studying the genetics of elephants is obviously not a very good idea if even that of fruit flies remains obscure. Indeed, one of us has suggested elsewhere that this explanatory impotence may well be caused by overly simplistic ideas about individual-level voting, traceable to political sociology's long-standing class theory of politics (Houtman 2003: 103-120). Studies of the relationship between class and voting are after all still typically based on the assumption that voters are inclined to vote for "the natural party of their class" (Heath et al. 1995: 564), i.e., the party that represents their "true class interests" (Lipset 1970: 186). Due to its weak economic position, then, the working class is assumed to favor economic redistribution and hence vote for leftist parties, whereas due to its privileged economic position the middle class is assumed to dislike economic redistribution and hence vote for rightist ones. In this long-standing theoretical tradition, in short, voting is conceived of as the expression of a "democratic class struggle" (Lipset 1960: 220, see also Nieuwbeerta 1995: 1).

Something seems seriously wrong with this theoretical heritage, however. Why else would it be so strikingly impotent in explaining why the familiar alignments have declined in the first place and why they are weaker in some countries than in others? And indeed, how "true" are those class interests and how "natural" an ally are the leftist parties if the working class increasingly votes for parties that contradict its class-based economic interests? In this first empirical chapter, in short, we need to face the theoretical problem squarely and open-mindedly: How to explain "unnatural" voting, i.e., voting that *contradicts* one's "true" class interests?

A Cultural Explanation for "Unnatural" Voting

Free-Floating Theoretical Interpretations

Since the Marxist notion of "false class consciousness" has lost its former credibility, various authors have suggested that class-based economic motivations may also account for rightist votes by the working class. Reid (1977: 232), for instance, suggests that workers, because of their weak position on the labor market, are burdened by immigrants who compete with them for scarce jobs. They are hence held to have a class interest in restricting immigration and voting for rightist parties. In a similar vein, Weakliem and Heath (1994: 246-247) suggest that workers may also serve their class-based economic interests by voting for rightist parties, because this enables them to profit from higher levels of long-term economic growth.

Suggestions such as those aim at forcing the phenomenon of a rightist-voting working class into the straightjacket of the class theory of politics by stretching the notion of class-based economic interests. Although there is nothing wrong in itself about interpreting new facts with the help of existing theories, this strategy becomes problematical if, as in those two examples, inventing theoretical interpretations without applying any empirical tests is all that is done. Empirical backup is required before one can legitimately pigeonhole working-class rightist voting as driven by class-based economic interests as well. This empirical backup does however not exist in these instances.

Economic interests are also stretched analytically to account for middle-class leftist voting. In the so-called theory of the "New Class," leftist voting members of the middle class are also assumed to pursue their class-based economic interests (Bruce-Briggs 1979, Brint 1984, De Graaf and Steijn 1997). Because they are typically occupied in government service, they are held to benefit from government interference because this provides them with jobs and career opportunities. Again, those class interests exist by definitional fiat only so that class-based economic interests are stretched considerably without proper direct empirical tests being conducted (see Bell 1980 and Horowitz 1984 for a critical discussion of theories of an alleged "New Class").

This stretching of class interests merely underlines the dominance of class analysis in political sociology. Even though classes increasingly vote for the "wrong" parties, the logic of class analysis itself is not called into question, but rather applied more leniently so as to be able to incorporate the deviant cases and hence "maintain the established theoretical order" (Houtman 2003: 163). In this way, a gradual immunization of the class theory of politics takes place. If workers vote for leftist parties, this is because they pursue their class interests; if they vote for rightist ones, this is also because they pursue their class interests. Whatever the empirical findings one arrives at during one's studies, in short, one can in retrospect always claim that the class theory of politics succeeds in explaining voting behavior.

Class, Cultural Capital, and Political Values

This one-sided focus on class-based economic interests and economic voting motives is remarkable, because Lipset has already pointed to culturally rightist tendencies in the working class in the 1950s. In his influential article "Democracy and Working-Class Authoritarianism" (1959) he introduced a distinction between economic values relating to the distribution of wealth and income and cultural values relating to individual liberty and social order and argued that the working class is characterized by a combination of economic egalitarianism (in favor of economic redistribution) and authoritarianism (Lipset 1959: 485). On the other hand, Inglehart (1977, 1990, 1997) has pointed out culturally leftist tendencies in the middle class, characterized by him as a "postmaterialist" emphasis on individual liberty and self-attainment (see also Kriesi 1998). Working-class authoritarianism, characterized by an emphasis on social order, and middle-class postmaterialism, characterized by an emphasis on individual freedom, prove each other's mirror images (see e.g., Middendorp 1991: 262, Dekker et al. 1999, Houtman 2003: 66-82) and in this book, we refer to this broad complex of moral and political values, that also includes those pertaining to gender, sexual, and parental roles, as authoritarianism/libertarianism (compare Middendorp 1991, Houtman 2003).

The social scientific literature concerning authoritarianism/libertarianism features a strong consensus that authoritarianism is caused by a low level of education rather than a low income (see for instance Lipsitz 1965, Grabb 1979, 1980, Dekker and Ester 1987, Houtman 2001, 2003: 24-46, 2004). Much less consensus, however, exists about whether or not this effect of education can be interpreted as a class effect. On the one hand, there are those who argue that it can, because education is widely considered a key class indicator (see on the latter point, e.g., Goldthorpe 1980, Lipset 1981, Wright 1985). On the other hand, there are those who argue that, although education and class are obviously strongly correlated, they cannot be equated (e.g., Grabb 1979, 1980, Dekker and Ester 1987). Indeed, Inglehart suggests that the postmaterialism of the well educated cannot be interpreted as a class effect, because variables such as occupation and income do not have similar effects on postmaterialism (1977: 72-89).[1]

The key question, then, is whether or not the libertarianism of the highly educated confirms the theory that authoritarianism, just like economic egalitarianism, can be explained from a weak class position. Lamont (1986) proposes instead that cultural capital—i.e., the ability to recognize cultural expressions and comprehend their meaning (Bourdieu 1984, 1986)—is decisive. This is a promising suggestion for three reasons. First, since Bourdieu's path-breaking work in this area, education is today no longer merely considered a key indicator for the strength of one's labor market position, but for cultural capital as well (see, for example, Kalmijn 1994, De Graaf and Kalmijn 2001). Second, the validity of education as an indicator for cultural capital is underscored by its substantial positive correlation with cultural participation (see for instance DiMaggio 1982, DiMaggio and Mohr 1985). Indeed, Bourdieu (1986) makes a distinction between education as an indicator for institutionalized cultural capital and cultural participation as an indicator for embodied cultural capital.

Third, although the notion of cultural capital is typically used in studies of school success, social mobility, and reproduction of social inequality (e.g., DiMaggio 1982, DiMaggio and Mohr 1985, Niehof 1997), it also makes sense theoretically to assume that it affects libertarianism (see also Gabennesch 1972). This is because it is likely that cultural capital stimulates an appreciation of social orders as "socially constructed" and hence erodes belief in "natural" or "pre-given" ones. This "denaturalizing" tendency fosters alienation and hence appreciation of individual liberty and acceptance of cultural diversity to an extent not typically found among those who lack cultural capital. The latter are more likely to evaluate unfamiliar modes of living as morally reprehensible deviations from a "natural" order, fostering anomie and sympathy for authoritarian attempts aimed at re-establishing the latter (Houtman 2003: 27-28; see 152-164 for a comparison with Bourdieu's concept of cultural capital).

In short, the question what the relationship between education and authoritarianism/libertarianism actually means, cannot be answered by an assessment of the statistical effects of variables such as occupational class and/or education. Occupational class inevitably mixes up the strength of one's labor market position with the amount of cultural capital as indicated by education. It thus inevitably produces a "working class" with a weak economic position and a limited amount of cultural capital and a middle class with a strong economic position and ample cultural capital. In a similar vein, education also has an economic and a cultural face, typically referred to as "human capital" and "cultural capital," respectively. To bypass the problems of theoretical interpretation posed by the use of theoretically ambiguous variables such as these, it is necessary to use more explicit indicators for class and cultural capital.

We use wage dependence, risk of unemployment, and income to measure the strength of one's class position and cultural participation to measure cultural capital. We hence expect education to have a similar effect on economic egalitarianism as these three explicit class indicators. More specifically, we expect a weaker class position—and hence a lower level of education—to lead to stronger economic egalitarianism. On the other hand, we expect education to have a similar effect on authoritarianism as cultural participation, with more of both producing stronger libertarianism.

Hypotheses

The above leads us to expect that cultural capital rather than class-based economic interests is decisive in explaining "unnatural" voting. More specifically, we expect members of the working class to adhere to authoritarian values that lead them to cast rightist votes, because they only have a limited amount of cultural capital. For members of the middle class, we expect exactly the reverse. Because of their larger amount of cultural capital, they are expected to adhere predominantly to culturally libertarian values that lead them to vote for leftist parties. As to leftist-voting members of the working class and rightist-voting members of the middle class ("natural" voting), the explanation offered by traditional class analysis, drawing on economic class interests, is of course expected to be tenable.

What we expect, in short, is that class-based economic interests and cultural capital have contradictory consequences for voting behavior. If people vote consistent with their class-based economic interests ("natural" voting), we expect this to be caused by the strengths of their class positions and the economically egalitarian or conservative values these give rise to. If they vote inconsistent with their class-based economic interests ("unnatural" voting), we expect this to be caused by their amounts of cultural capital and the authoritarian or libertarian values connected to these.

Data and Measurement

Income. We use net monthly family income and hence combine each respondent's income with that of his or her partner. We distinguish ten income categories: 1 (Dfl. 0 to Dfl. 999), 2 (Dfl. 1,000 to Dfl. 1,999) etc. through 10 (Dfl. 9,000 or higher).[2]

Wage dependence. Wage dependence has simply been measured by asking all working respondents whether or not they are in salaried employment. Answers were no (1), and yes (2).

Risk of unemployment. Risk of unemployment has been measured by asking 1) whether or not respondents had a temporary contract, 2) the number of times the respondent had been unemployed for a period longer than three months since the completion of full-time education, and 3) an estimation of the risk that a person with the same job and the same type of contract (either temporary or permanent) would be forced to look for another job within the next three years. After standardizing the answers to these three questions, they have been combined into a scale ranging from zero to ten. Factor analysis produces only one factor with an eigenvalue higher than one, explaining 54 percent of the total variance, and the scale's reliability is 0.67 (Cronbach's α). Higher scale scores indicate higher risks of unemployment.

Economic egalitarianism/conservatism has been measured by means of six Likert-type items that state, for example, that the government should take measures to reduce income differences and that large income differences are unjust because in principle all people are equal. The reader is referred to Table 6.1 in Chapter 6 below for the full set of items. Factor analysis produces a single factor with an eigenvalue higher than one, explaining 41 percent of the variance. The reliability of the scale is 0.71 (Cronbach's α) and high scores indicate economic egalitarianism.

Authoritarianism/libertarianism has been measured by means of a short version of the F-scale for authoritarianism (Adorno et al. 1950), a scale measuring acceptance/rejection of traditional gender roles, a scale measuring expressive/instrumental educational orientations, and Inglehart's index for postmaterialism. The reader is referred to Table 6.1 in Chapter 6 below for the F-scale items and to Houtman (2003: 73-77) for the other sets of items. Factor analysis produces one factor with an eigenvalue higher than one, explaining 53 percent of the variance. Factor loadings are -0.82 for authoritarianism, 0.69 for rejection of traditional gender roles, 0.74 for an expressive educational orientation, and 0.65 for postmaterialism. The latter three measures have been reversed and then linearly combined with the F-scale scores in such a way that high scores indicate authoritarianism.

Cultural participation has been measured by asking each respondent the number of books he or she owned, the number of novels he or she had read in the previous three months, the number of times he or she had been to concerts, the theatre, cabaret, or ballet and art exhibitions, the frequency with which he or she speaks with others about art and culture, and the extent to which he or she regards him- or herself as "a lover of arts and culture." Factor analysis produces one factor with an eigenvalue higher than one that explains 45 percent of the variance. The reliability of the scale is 0.79 (Cronbach's α) and higher scores indicate more cultural participation (see for details: Houtman 2003: 34).

Education. Seven levels of education have been distinguished: 1) no more than elementary education: 2.7 percent; 2) lower vocational education: 15.0 percent; 3) advanced special education: 13.6 percent; 4) five- or six-year secondary education: 9.0 percent; 5) intermediary vocational education: 22.6 percent; 6) higher vocational education (BA): 26.3 percent; 7) university education (MA): 8.0 percent. As expected, and consistent with the findings by others discussed above, education is strongly and positively related to cultural participation ($r=0.41$, $p<0.001$, one-tailed test). This substantial correlation underscores that education taps not only into the strength of one's labor market position, but into cultural capital, too.

Voting behavior. The respondents have been asked which party they would vote for if there were elections for the Dutch Parliament on the next day. Respondents who indicated that they would vote for the Labor Party (PVDA), the Greens (GroenLinks) or the Socialist Party (SP) were classified as left. Respondents who indicated that they would vote for the Conservative Party (VVD), the Democrats (D66), Christian Democrats (CDA), or one of three small fundamentalist Christian parties (SGP/GPV/RPF) were coded non-left. Respondents who indicated that they would

Table 2.1
Frequency Distribution of EGP Class Schema (N=711)

EGP class		%
Class I	Higher-grade professionals, self-employed or salaried, higher-grade administrators and officials in central and local government and in public and private enterprises; managers in large industrial establishments; large proprietors.	15.0
Class II	Lower grade professionals and higher grade technicians; lower grade administrators and officials; managers in small business and industrial establishments and in services; supervisors of nonmanual employees.	30.2
Class III	Routine nonmanual workers: clerical workers, sales personnel, and other rank and file employees in services.	21.2
Class IV	Petty bourgeoisie: small proprietors, including farmers and smallholders; self-employed artisans and all other "own account" workers apart from professionals.	5.3
Class V	Supervisors of manual workers and lower grade technicians.	7.5
Class VI	Skilled manual workers in all branches of industry.	5.8
Class VII	Semi and unskilled manual workers in industry and agricultural workers.	14.2
Unknown		0.7
Total		100.0

not vote or would vote for (small) parties not mentioned here, were left out of the analysis.

Class. To introduce a distinction between "unnatural" and "natural" voters, we use the EGP-class schema, designed by Erikson, Goldthorpe, and Portocarero (1979). Seven different class positions are assigned on the basis of 1) occupational title, 2) whether or not one is self-employed, and 3) the number of employees one supervises (Erikson and Goldthorpe 1992: 38-39, Bakker et al. 1997: 8). Table 2.1 shows the distribution of the 711 respondents working at least 20 hours to whom we assigned EGP-class positions.

The seven EGP classes do not constitute a simple hierarchy (Goldthorpe 1980: 42). Although the three nonmanual classes—higher professionals (Class I), lower professionals (Class II), and nonmanual workers (Class IV)—and the three manual ones (Class V, Class VI, and Class VII) constitute two separate hierarchies, the hierarchical relationship between these two is undetermined. The same goes for the relationship between each of those hierarchies and the petty bourgeoisie (Class IV). The higher professionals (Class I), the lower professionals (Class II), and the petty bourgeoisie (Class

Table 2.2
Leftist Voting Behavior Explained by EGP Class Position
("unnatural" voting behavior emphasized, N "natural" voters=304,
N "unnatural" voters=233)

EGP class	Non-left	Left
Higher professionals (I)	56.0	*44.0*
Lower professionals (II)	62.4	*37.6*
Nonmanual workers (III)	55.0	*45.0*
Petty bourgeoisie (IV)	81.8	*18.2*
Higher working class (V)	*61.0*	39.0
Skilled manual workers (VI)	*57.7*	42.3
Semi and unskilled manual workers (VII)	*52.4*	47.6
Total	59.6	40.4

Cramer's V=0.14 (p>0.10)

IV) can be classified unambiguously as middle class, while the classes of skilled manual workers (Class VI) and semi and unskilled manual workers (Class VII) are part of the working class.

Assigning Classes III and V to either working class or middle class is more contestable, however. Class V consists of lower-grade technicians and supervisors of manual workers. Although it may as such be distinguished from the working class "proper" as "a latter-day aristocracy of labour or a "blue collar" élite" (Goldthorpe 1980: 41), we follow Andersen and Heath (2002) and Nieuwbeerta (1995) here and consider Class V (with Classes VI and VII) part of the working class.[3] Although one may in a similar vein argue that the least privileged nonmanual class, i.e., that of the nonmanual workers (Class III), consists of "white collar proletarians" (e.g., Wright 1979) and hence needs to be distinguished from the middle class "proper," we nevertheless consider Class III part of the middle class here (with Classes I, II, and IV).[4]

Results

Distinguishing "Natural" from "Unnatural" Voters

Table 2.2 shows the preferences of members of the seven EGP classes for left and non-left political parties. It is clear that, on the basis of knowledge of one's class position, no predictions can be made about the party one would most likely vote for (Cramer's V=0.14, p>0.10). That the working class is just as likely as the middle class to vote for a rightist party merely underscores the importance of the theoretical problem addressed in this chapter.

In order to explain why so many members of the middle class vote left and why so many members of the working class vote right, we distinguish "unnatural" from "natural" voters. All members of the working class who say they will vote for a non-leftist party and all members of the middle class who say they will vote for a leftist one are thus placed in the category of "unnatural" voters. We code as "natural" voters all members of the working class who say they will vote for a leftist party and all members of the middle class who say they will vote for a non-leftist one.

Because the dependent variable in our analyses has only two values, left and non-left, we apply logistic regression analysis to find out whether, as expected, the logic of class analysis applies only to the "natural" voters, while "unnatural" voting stems from cultural capital and authoritarianism/libertarianism. We omit EGP class from our analysis, because including it would be meaningless. Because it has already been used to

Table 2.3
"Natural" Voting Explained
(1=non-left, 2=left, log-odds ratios with standard errors in parentheses, N=281)

Independent variables	Model 1	Model 2	Model 3
Risk of unemployment	0.09 (0.09)		0.03 (0.10)
Wage dependence	2.23* (1.12)		1.19 (1.14)
Income	-0.41** (0.15)		-0.13 (0.16)
Education	-0.73*** (0.13)		-0.70*** (0.14)
Cultural participation	-0.13 (0.23)		-0.37 (0.25)
Economic egalitarianism		1.61*** (0.27)	1.22*** (0.31)
Authoritarianism		0.16 (0.24)	-0.50 (0.31)
Constant	1.37 (1.34)	-6.96 (1.22)	-0.39 (2.18)
-2 Log likelihood	197.44	227.15	176.55
Pseudo R^2 (Nagelkerke)	0.39	0.25	0.47

* $p<0.05$; ** $p<0.01$; *** $p<0.001$

code respondents into the two categories of voters, its inclusion would produce perfect explanations for both types of voters. All members of the working class in the category of "natural" voters would vote for leftist parties and all members of the middle class for rightist ones. Reversely, all members of the working class among the "unnatural" voters vote for a rightist party and all members of the middle class for a leftist one. Including EGP class as an independent variable would also be theoretically meaningless, because we have already seen above that EGP class does not affect the vote. More than that, it is this very circumstance that underscores the relevance of the problem addressed in this chapter.

Explaining "Natural" Voting

Table 2.3 contains three statistical models addressing the explanation of "natural" voting. The first model estimates the effects of the indicators of class and cultural capital on voting behavior, the second those of economic egalitarianism/conservatism and authoritarianism/libertarianism, and the third those of all of these variables together.

The two unambiguously cultural variables (cultural participation and authoritarianism/libertarianism) play no role whatsoever for the "natural" voters. The indicators of the strength of one's labor market position, however, affect voting behavior. In the first model, we find significant effects for wage dependence and for family income. For wage-dependent "natural" voters the odds of voting left are higher than for those who are not wage dependent, and for those with lower family incomes the odds of doing so are higher than for those with higher family incomes. These effects disappear after controlling for economic egalitarianism in the third model. This means that a weak position on the labor market leads to economic egalitarianism, which in turn leads to higher odds of voting left. A lower level of education also increases the odds of voting for a leftist party. Like the effects of wage dependence and income, this effect of educational level also needs to be understood as a consequence of class-based economic interests.

The final model explains no less than 50 percent of the variance of "natural" voting and it is hence clear that "natural" voting can very well be explained from class-based economic interests. This is not a surprising finding at all, of course, because it is exactly what the class theory of politics has been assuming all along. The importance of this finding becomes clear, however, when we next look at the results of a similar type of analysis for the "unnatural" voters.

Table 2.4
"Unnatural" Voting Explained
(1=non-left, 2=left, log-odds ratios with standard errors in parentheses, N=218)

Independent variables	Model 1	Model 2	Model 3
Risk of unemployment	0.13 (0.09)		0.09 (0.10)
Wage dependence	-5.56 (16.17)		-5.70 (15.96)
Income	0.15 (0.13)		0.19 (0.00)
Education	0.46*** (0.12)		0.34** (0.13)
Cultural participation	0.85*** (0.21)		0.44 (0.24)
Economic egalitarianism		0.31 (0.25)	0.49 (0.27)
Authoritarianism		-1.84*** (0.28)	-1.15*** (0.34)
Constant	3.58 (16.19)	5.71*** (1.24)	6.17 (16.12)
-2 Log likelihood	200.24	200.50	179.41
Pseudo R^2 (Nagelkerke)	0.38	0.37	0.47

* $p<0.05$; ** $p<0.01$; *** $p<0.001$

Explaining "Unnatural" Voting

Risk of unemployment, wage dependence, family income, and economic egalitarianism, all class-related variables, play no role whatsoever in explaining "unnatural" voting. The effect of cultural participation, however, is significant and positive in the first model, indicating higher odds of voting left for those who are more culturally active. This effect disappears after controlling for authoritarianism in the third model, in which the negative effect of authoritarianism indicates that culturally libertarian people are more inclined to vote for leftist parties. This means that, as expected, people with a larger amount of cultural capital are more libertarian, which increases the odds of voting for a party on the left. The effect of level of education is significant and positive in the first as well as the third model, which needs to be understood in a cultural sense. It indicates that the odds of voting for a leftist party increase as the educational level of the "unnatural" voters increases. This effect clearly contrasts with the effect of education found in our analysis for the "natural" voters.

Note that the final model explains about 50 percent of the variance of "unnatural" voting, closely resembling the percentage found for "natural" voting. This means that the cultural explanation of voting behavior fits the "unnatural" voters just as well as the class-based explanation fits the "natural" ones. Unlike "natural" voting, in short, "unnatural" voting can be explained from cultural capital and the cultural values connected to it.

The role of education in both analyses deserves some comments. Its effect is negative among "natural" voters, but positive among "unnatural" voters. This convincingly underscores the ambiguous nature of education as an indicator of class and cultural capital simultaneously. It is also remarkable that the direct effects of education on voting behavior disappear in neither analysis after economic and cultural values are controlled for. This suggests that voting is not only value-rationally motivated (i.e., driven by economic egalitarianism/conservatism and authoritarianism/libertarianism), but that economic and cultural identities related to economic and cultural positions (both indicated by education) play a role as well (compare Weakliem and Heath 1994).

To sum up our findings, "natural" voters base their votes on economic motives that flow from their class-based economic interests. Precisely as they are traditionally taken to be, working-class votes for the left and middle-class votes for the right are thus caused by economic voting motivations that result from one's class-based economic interests. These interests do not drive the behavior of "unnatural" voters, however. Rightist-voting members of the working class and leftist-voting members of the middle class vote the way they do, because of cultural voting motivations that are connected to cultural capital. "Natural" voting is basically *class voting* and "unnatural" voting *cultural voting*, in short.

Class Voting and Cultural Voting in the Netherlands, 2002

The importance of the distinction between class voting and cultural voting can further be demonstrated by means of an analysis of patterns of voting during the by now historical Dutch parliamentary elections of May 2002. These elections witnessed the tumultuous rise of Pim Fortuyn's rightist-populist LPF that won 17 percent of the votes, after having already collected no less than 35 percent of the votes in the local elections in Rotterdam in March of that same year. Until these elections in 2002, rightist-populist parties had remained remarkably marginal in the Netherlands, in sharp contrast to countries such as Belgium (Vlaams Blok; Vlaams Belang since 2004), France (Front National), Austria (FPÖ), Denmark (People's Party), and Italy (Alleanza Nazionale and Lega Nord). Although the rightist-extremist Centre Party (later on: Centre Democrats) had managed to mobilize some electoral support in the Netherlands during the 1980s, this was very limited indeed.

While the emergence of the New Left in the Netherlands by and large coincided with that in countries such as France (Les Verts) and West Germany (Die Grünen) (Inglehart 1990: 281-283, Hoffman Martinot 1991),[5] the parliamentary elections of 2002 thus finally witnessed the electoral breakthrough of the New Right in the Netherlands, too. Just like the new-leftist Greens (GroenLinks), the new-rightist Populist Party (LPF) does not so much present itself through issues concerning economic distribution, but rather through cultural ones. Whereas the Greens (GroenLinks) strongly emphasize the value of individual liberty and hence the rights of traditionally excluded cultural minority groups, the Populist Party (LPF) instead emphasizes the necessity of maintaining social order in the nation, especially by means of strict cultural assimilation of Muslim migrants. Both parties thus differ from the Labor Party (PVDA) and the Conservative Party (VVD), the two large parties that have in the Netherlands traditionally represented the economic interests of the working class and the (upper) middle class, respectively.

As such, the Dutch parliamentary elections of 2002 offer a perfect opportunity to study whether voting for old-leftist and old-rightist parties indeed needs to be understood as class voting, while voting for new-leftist and new-rightist ones rather stands out as cultural voting. We analyze the Dutch data of the *European Social Survey* (2002) to find this out, restricting our analysis to those respondents who say they would vote for the new-leftist Greens (GroenLinks), the new-rightist Populist Party (LPF), the old-leftist Labor Party (PVDA), and the old-rightist Conservative Party (VVD). We assign EGP class positions to all respondents with an occupation[6] by means of a coding procedure that has been developed by Ganzeboom and Treiman (2005) and we distinguish six different levels of education.[7] We could measure authoritarianism/libertarianism with no less than eight items,[8] but due to data limitations, we could rely on no more than two items for the measurement of economic egalitarianism/conservatism.[9]

When we lump together Old Left with New Left and Old Right with New Right, we find a pattern that is very much like that in Table 2.2 above. Table 2.5 points out that although manual workers are more likely to vote for a Leftist party, the difference is only very slight indeed. If we fail to distinguish Old Left from New Left and Old Right from New Right, EGP class can explain no more than two percent of the differences in voting behavior.

Again, however, we cannot conclude from this that the class theory of politics has become obsolete. Conceiving of voting as driven by class-based economic interests, it works perfectly well when it comes to explaining votes for either the old-leftist Labor Party (PVDA) or the old-rightist Conservative Party (VVD). As Table 2.6 points out, after all, the odds of voting for the Labor Party are highest for those with the most precarious economic positions—skilled and unskilled manual workers as well as the poorly educated—while those with more favorable economic positions tend to vote for the Conservative Party (VVD). This difference in voting behavior is moreover caused by stronger desires for economic redistribution among the former as compared to the latter, precisely as the class theory of politics predicts. It is abundantly clear, in short, that voting for the old-leftist Labor Party (PVDA) and the old-rightist Conservative Party (VVD) can be characterized as class voting: class-based economic interests are decisive here.

The picture changes dramatically when we attempt to explain votes for the new-leftist Greens (GroenLinks) and the new-rightist Populist Party (LPF), however (Table 2.7). Although the poorly educated tend to vote for the Populist Party (LPF) and the well educated for the Greens (GroenLinks), distinctions between EGP classes have no explanatory

Table 2.5
Voting for a Rightist or Leftist Party Explained (1=right, 2=left, log-odds ratios with standard errors in parentheses, N=972)

Independent variables	
Higher professionals (I)[1]	--
Lower professionals (II)	0.07
	(0.18)
Nonnmanual workers (III)	0.14
	(0.23)
Petty bourgeoisie (IV)	-0.47
	(0.36)
Higher working class (V)	-0.01
	(0.34)
Skilled manual workers (VI)	0.70*
	(0.33)
Semi and unskilled manual workers (VII)	0.71**
	(0.25)
Education	0.05
	(0.04)
Constant	-0.53*
	(0.27)
Pseudo R^2 (Nagelkerke)	0.02

*$p<0.05$; **$p<0.01$; ***$p<0.001$
1. Not included in analysis (reference category)

value whatsoever in this case. And indeed, the votes for the Populist Party (LPF) by the poorly educated and for the Greens (GroenLinks) by the well educated are driven by high levels of authoritarianism and libertarianism, respectively, underscoring that education plays a cultural rather than an economic role here. Economic egalitarianism also leads to voting for the Greens (GroenLinks), to be sure, but its role is substantially weaker. Moreover, the circumstance that it leads the well educated rather than the poorly educated to vote for a leftist party obviously flies in the face of the class theory of politics.

Table 2.6
Voting for the Old-Rightist Conservative Party (VVD) or the Old-Leftist Labor Party (PVDA) Explained
(1=Conservative Party, 2=Labor Party, log-odds ratios with standard errors in parentheses, N=580)

Independent variables	Model 1	Model 2	Model 3	Model 4
Higher professionals (I)[1]	--	--	--	--
Lower professionals (II)	0.20 (0.23)	-0.05 (0.26)	0.19 (0.24)	-0.05 (0.26)
Nonnmanual workers (III)	0.04 (0.30)	-0.18 (0.33)	0.02 (0.30)	-0.18 (0.33)
Petty bourgeoisie (IV)	-0.68 (0.48)	-0.94 (0.52)	-0.78 (0.49)	-1.03 (0.53)
Higher working class (V)	0.25 (0.45)	0.35 (0.54)	0.20 (0.46)	0.27 (0.54)
Skilled manual workers (VI)	1.25** (0.49)	0.93 (0.54)	1.32** (0.49)	1.01 (0.54)
Semi and unskilled manual workers (VII)	1.14** (0.36)	0.78 (0.40)	1.19** (0.37)	0.81* (0.40)
Education	-0.24* (0.11)	-0.04 (0.07)	-0.19** (0.06)	-0.19 (0.13)
Economic egalitarianism		1.30*** (0.14)		1.31*** (0.15)
Authoritarianism			-0.46*** (0.13)	-0.47** (0.15)
Constant	-0.03 (0.19)	0.40 (0.40)	-0.62 (0.48)	-1.17* (0.49)
Pseudo R^2 (Nagelkerke)	0.10	0.32	0.13	0.34

*p<0.05; **p<0.01; ***p<0.001
1. Not included in analysis (reference category)

Table 2.7
Voting for the New-Rightist Populist Party (LPF) or the New-Leftist Greens (GroenLinks) (1=Populist Party, 2= Greens, log-odds ratios with standard errors in parentheses, N=392)

Independent variables	Model 1	Model 2	Model 3	Model 4
Higher professionals (I)[1]	--	--	--	--
Lower professionals (II)	-0.04 (0.31)	-0.06 (0.32)	0.03 (0.37)	-0.07 (0.39)
Nonnmanual workers (III)	0.58 (0.38)	0.45 (0.39)	0.61 (0.44)	0.46 (0.46)
Petty bourgeoisie (IV)	-0.30 (0.58)	-0.06 (0.60)	-0.25 (0.69)	0.06 (0.73)
Higher working class (V)	-0.30 (0.59)	-0.51 (0.60)	-0.44 (0.69)	-0.62 (0.70)
Skilled manual workers (VI)	-0.83 (0.75)	-1.25 (0.77)	-0.21 (0.80)	-0.54 (0.82)
Semi and unskilled manual workers (VII)	0.51 (0.41)	0.45 (0.43)	0.32 (0.47)	0.25 (0.50)
Education	0.71*** (0.15)	0.46*** (0.08)	0.24** (0.09)	0.59*** (0.18)
Economic egalitarianism		0.77*** (0.16)		0.87*** (0.21)
Authoritarianism			-1.73*** (0.21)	-1.75*** (0.14)
Constant	-0.89** (0.26)	-2.70*** (0.51)	-6.96*** (0.83)	-6.05*** (0.73)
Pseudo R^2 (Nagelkerke)	0.11	0.20	0.42	0.48

*p<0.05; **p<0.01; ***p<0.001
1. Not included in analysis (reference category)

These findings confirm, in short, that voting for the new-leftist Greens (GroenLinks) and the new-rightist Populist Party (LPF) indeed cannot be understood as class voting, but rather constitutes cultural voting. While it is perfectly able to explain votes for old-leftist and old-rightist parties, then, the class theory of politics has nothing to offer when it comes to the explanation of votes for new-leftist and new-rightist parties.

Conclusion

Relying on insights that depart from the theoretical heritage of the class theory of politics, we have developed, tested, and confirmed a supplementary cultural explanation for voting behavior in this chapter. Whereas the strength of one's economic position produces votes that are consistent with one's class-based economic interests, cultural capital accounts for votes that contradict the latter. Whereas the former, "natural" voting, thus constitutes class voting, the latter, "unnatural" voting, entails cultural voting. Voting for old-leftist and old-rightist parties, which both primarily emphasize the good-old class-related issues of economic distribution, proves still very well understandable as class voting. Voting for new-leftist and new-rightist parties, which both primarily emphasize issues pertaining to individual liberty and maintenance of social order, however, rather proves to entail cultural voting. With its one-sided focus on class-based economic interests, in short, the class theory of politics is disturbingly ill-equipped to explain why an increasing part of the working class votes for rightist parties today.

The demonstrated need to distinguish class voting from cultural voting implies that a negligible relationship between class position and voting behavior does not necessarily mean that "class hardly affects the vote," as political sociologists have traditionally tended to conclude. It may after all also mean that class voting is by and large cancelled out—or better said, made invisible—by about equally strong cultural voting working in the reverse direction. And indeed, this is exactly what we have demonstrated for the Netherlands in this chapter: although there is hardly any relationship to be found between class position and voting behavior, class-based economic interests nevertheless still strongly drive the vote these days. As we have also demonstrated in the present chapter, however, this only becomes visible to the social-scientific observer if cultural voting is systematically distinguished from class voting.

From a theoretical point of view, our findings so far point out that the rightist-voting working class is likely to remain an unresolved theoretical puzzle as long as students of political behavior neglect the cultural dynamics that underlie "unnatural" voting. We therefore push our analysis further forward by addressing the vital question raised by our findings so far: Why exactly do some voters comply with the logic of class voting and others with that of cultural voting? More specifically: what role does an alleged new political culture in which cultural issues are held to have increasingly replaced the old issues of class have to play in this? It is this question that we address in the next two chapters.

Notes

1. Note, however, that Inglehart's alternative interpretation of this effect—as stemming from parental affluence—is not empirically sustained either (compare Houtman 2003: 66-82).
2. Dfl. 1000 equals approximately 450 euros. The Dutch guilder was replaced by the euro on January 1, 2002.
3. Conceiving of Class V as part of either working class or middle class does not substantially change the findings of this chapter.
4. Conceiving of Class III as part of either working class or middle class does not substantially change the findings of this chapter.
5. The Radical Party (PPR) was founded in 1968 and by that time the popularity of the Pacifist Party (PSP, already founded in 1957) also increased strongly. These two parties later on merged with the former Communist Party (CPN), which had itself changed unrecognizably due to the influence of the new spirit of the time, into the new party GroenLinks in 1989. GroenLinks has ever since remained the only new-leftist party of considerable size in the Netherlands.
6. We relied on either present occupation or last occupation (if retired or unemployed).
7. These six categories are: 1) no more than elementary education; 2) lower vocational education (LBO, VMBO) or four-year secondary education (MULO, MAVO); 3) intermediary vocational education (MBO) or five-year secondary education (HAVO); 4) pre-university education (HBS, VWO, Gymnasium); 5) higher vocational education (BA); 6) university education (MA).
8. These eight questions are: "Important to do what is told and follow rules," "Important to behave properly," "Important to follow traditions and customs" (all three with six response categories), "Gays and lesbians free to live as they wish," "Better for a country if almost everyone shares customs and traditions" (both with five response categories), "Country's cultural life undermined or enriched by immigrants," "Immigrants make country worse or better place to live," and "Immigrants make countries" crime problems worse or better" (all three with five response categories). Principal component analysis produces a first factor with seven factor loadings between 0.45 and 0.67 and one (that on gays and lesbians) of 0.28. This first factor explains somewhat more than 30 percent of the variance: certainly not spectacular, but enough to construct a modestly reliable scale (Cronbach's α = 0.64). Scores have been assigned as the means of the standardized items.
9. Both are Likert-type items: "The government should take measures to reduce income differences" and "Employees need strong trade unions to protect their working conditions and wages" (both with five response categories indicating the degree of (dis)agreement). The correlation between the answers to the two questions is 0.30 and a principal component analysis produces a first factor that explains no less than 65 percent of the variance. Although this is substantial, with only two items it is impossible to construct a reliable scale (Cronbach's α remains limited to 0.46). Scores have been assigned as the means of the two standardized items.

3

A Cross-Pressured Working Class? Class Voting, Cultural Voting, and Issue Salience

Introduction

"A relation between class position and voting behavior is a natural and expected association in the Western democracies," Robert Alford argued in the 1960s: "Given the character of the stratification order and the way political parties act as representatives of different class interests, it would be remarkable if such a relation were not found" (1967: 68-69). And yet, precisely this "natural and expected" pattern of a leftist-voting working class and a rightist-voting middle class has declined considerably since World War II. There are a number of countries today where the relationship between class and voting is extremely weak or even completely absent. The United States is one striking example (Clark and Lipset 1991) and the Netherlands another, as we have seen in Chapter 2. A leftist-voting working class is less "natural" than the theoretical orthodoxy in political sociology maintains, in short.

Nevertheless, we have seen that working-class votes for the left and middle-class votes for the right can be explained in precisely the way the class theory of politics holds. "Unnatural" voting, however, is driven by a cultural rather than an economic voting motivation, stems from cultural capital rather than class, and leads the electorate to vote against its class-based economic interests. Whether people comply with the logic of either class voting or cultural voting is likely to depend on the political culture in which they find themselves, defined by the type of political issues that is salient (see for instance Baker et al. 1981, Clark 1998, 2001a, 2001b, Inglehart and Rabier 1986, Nieuwbeerta 2001). The first question we want to address in this chapter is therefore whether cultural issues have indeed become more salient and whether this means that class issues have become less so.

We do so by means of an analysis of data from the *American National Election Studies* (Sapiro et al. 2002). There are no compelling theoretical reasons for selecting the case of the United States, to be sure, because it conforms to the general pattern of a decline of a leftist-voting working class and a rightist-voting middle class that applies to most industrial democracies in the postwar era (Nieuwbeerta 1995, Weakliem and Heath 1999b; Manza and Brooks 1999). Our principal reason for selecting the case of the United States is that the *American National Election Studies*, unlike any other data source we are aware of, offers a unique opportunity to construct adequate measures for the salience of both types of issues for the full period 1960-2000.[1] Those data thus also enable us to study whether voters for whom cultural issues are salient are more likely to comply with the logic of cultural voting, while those for whom class issues are salient are more likely to comply with that of class voting.

The Coming of a New Political Culture?

From Class Issues to Cultural Issues?

Lipset's virtually generally accepted notion of voting as an expression of a "democratic class struggle" (1981) assumes a party system that entails an institutionalization of class interests and a political culture revolving around issues of economic distribution (Lipset 2001). The use of the word "labor" in the names of many leftist political parties, appealing to working-class interests, is one of the most visible manifestations of these tendencies (Robinson 1967). There is no doubt, of course, that the politics of most Western countries has traditionally been dominated by class conflict in the sense that issues tied to class inequality and economic distribution were at the heart of political debate. Many argue today, however, that the political culture has come to revolve less and less around class issues and has become "postmodern" (Inglehart 1997), "post-industrial" (Rempel and Clark 1997) or simply "new" (Clark 1998, 2001b) since the 1960s and 1970s, with the focus of attention shifting away from the "old" issues of class.

Although no agreement exists about the precise nature of the "new" issues (Pakulski 2001), they are generally conceived as "non-economic" (e.g., Clark 1998, 2001b, Heath et al. 1990, Rempel and Clark 1997). More precisely, new politics is mostly conceived of as left-libertarian politics, revolving around issues of expanding individual liberty, further democratization of society and enabling identities that were once defined as "deviant" to blossom freely (see e.g., Clark 1998, 2001b; McAllister and Studlar 1995). Without doubt, Inglehart's work on the spread of postmaterialist values constitutes the most influential example of this conception of new politics as new-leftist politics (1977, 1990, 1997). Inglehart started his studies into cultural and political change in the late 1960s to explain why middle-class youth, rather than the industrial working class, carried the torch of political protest. It is not odd at all that he conceived of new politics as new-leftist politics by then, emphasizing the "profound and fundamental disparities between the goals of the Postmaterialists and those of the Marxist left" (1990: 263-264). The counter culture and the new social movements that it spawned during the 1960s and 1970s *were* clear instances of left-libertarian politics, after all (e.g., Roszak 1969, Zijderveld 1970, Kriesi 1989, Kriesi and Van Praag 1987).

These left-libertarian movements, conceived by Inglehart (1977) as merely the most visible expressions of a more general "silent revolution," have not disappeared since, but have induced a right-authoritarian "silent counterrevolution" (Ignazi 1992, 2003, Veugelers 2000). Indeed, since the 1980s, new political parties at the rightist end of the new political spectrum blossom on authoritarian tendencies within the electorates of many European countries (see Elchardus 1996, Flanagan and Lee 2003, Swyngedouw 1994). Authors such as Hunter (1991) and Layman (2001) have pointed at a similar polarization concerning cultural issues in the United States, although principally revolving around the social role of religion and traditional moral values in this case. Although started as left-libertarian politics, in short, new politics today is more accurately characterized as a conflict between left-libertarian and right-authoritarian parties, movements and issues. "The point is that the New Right is as much *nonmaterialist* as the New Left," as Flanagan aptly summarizes the shortcoming of Inglehart's conceptualization of new politics (1987: 1308).

Although Inglehart and others fail to recognize that new politics, like class politics, consists of a right-authoritarian wing besides a left-libertarian one, it is hardly contested in the literature that cultural issues have become more salient during the last few decades (e.g., Inglehart 1977, 1987, 1990, 1997, Rempel and Clark 1997, Clark 1998 2001b; Hechter 2004, Pakulski and Waters 1996, Pakulski 2001). Our first hypothesis, derived from this theoretical consensus, leads us to expect that cultural issues have become more salient in the United States since 1960.

What Happens to the Old Issues of Class?

Inglehart assumes that the salience of the old issues of class declines as that of cultural ones increases, arguing that "the central element of the Marxist prescription, nationalization of industry, is almost a forgotten cause" (1997: 237) and that "economic cleavages did become less intense with rising levels of economic development, they gradually gave way to *other* types of conflict" (Inglehart 1997: 259). In his attempt to explain the decline of the relationship between class and voting from the class theory of politics, Nieuwbeerta (1995) also assumes that the salience of class issues has declined. Evans (1999b: 1) aptly summarizes the dominant position in the literature as follows:

> From being the "motor of history," the basis of the "democratic class struggle," class has for many become an outdated and increasingly irrelevant concept—more a part of "folk memory" than a currently significant phenomenon. The arguments of postmodernists and disillusioned socialists have been combined with those of the "end of ideology" liberals and numerous empirical researchers to assert that class inequality has lost its political importance.

The assumption that an increasing salience of cultural issues necessarily means that the salience of class issues has declined is not uncontested, however (e.g., Manza and Brooks 1996, Evans 2000). And indeed, authors who assume a decline of class issues always refer to the waning of hard-boiled socialist issues only. Inglehart (1997: 263), for instance, suggests that the recent neo-liberal upsurge and "the renewed respect for market forces that have emerged throughout most of the industrial world" mark the end of class politics. Inglehart thus neglects that rightist neo-liberal economic issues are also class issues, because they easily alienate the working class from the rightist parties to which it feels attracted because of its authoritarianism.

Notwithstanding speculations about what happens to the old issues of class when cultural issues become more salient, however, it is difficult to find even one empirical study that demonstrates convincingly that class issues (be it leftist or rightist ones) have indeed lost much of their former importance during the postwar period (compare Hechter 2004, Simmons 2004). We therefore study not only whether the salience of cultural issues has increased, but also whether that of class issues has waned.

Measuring Issue Salience

We measure issue salience by means of an open-ended question about what one considers the most important problem facing the country. Following Dunlap and Scarce (1991), Layman (2001) and Layman and Carmines (1997), we feel that answers to this question are a strong indicator for issue salience. Closely following the procedure by Layman and Carmines (1997: 765), respondents who choose a cultural or moral issue as the most important problem facing the country have been coded as being concerned with cultural issues.[2] Those who consider an issue of class inequality or economic distribution the most important problem facing the country have been coded as being concerned with class issues.[3] Because the number of conceivable problems facing the country is substantially larger than those two (it is virtually without limits, in fact), this obviously leaves us with a substantial category of respondents for whom neither cultural nor class issues are salient. The two resulting variables for class issue salience and cultural issue salience have been aggregated, so as to yield percentages for each of the twenty election years[4] during the period 1960-2000.

Figure 3.1 displays the development of cultural issue salience since 1960. It is evident that the political culture of the United States has changed significantly since 1960 in that the salience of cultural issues has increased strongly (r=0.58, p<0.01, one-sided test). This is consistent with the findings of Layman (2001: 33), who has demonstrated that in the period 1977-1996 American newspapers have come to pay increasing attention to cultural issues.

Figure 3.1
Cultural Issue Salience in the United States, 1960-2000

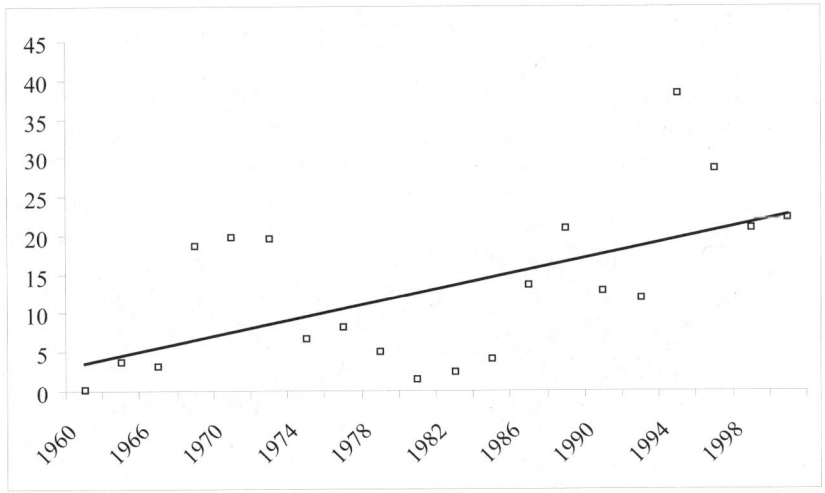

Inconsistent with the literature discussed above, however, the increase of cultural issue salience among the American population does not go at the cost of that of class issues. The salience of the latter has not declined at all during the period 1960-2000, but has remained remarkably constant (Figure 3.2, r=0.05, not significant).

Figure 3.2
Class Issue Salience in the United States, 1960-2000

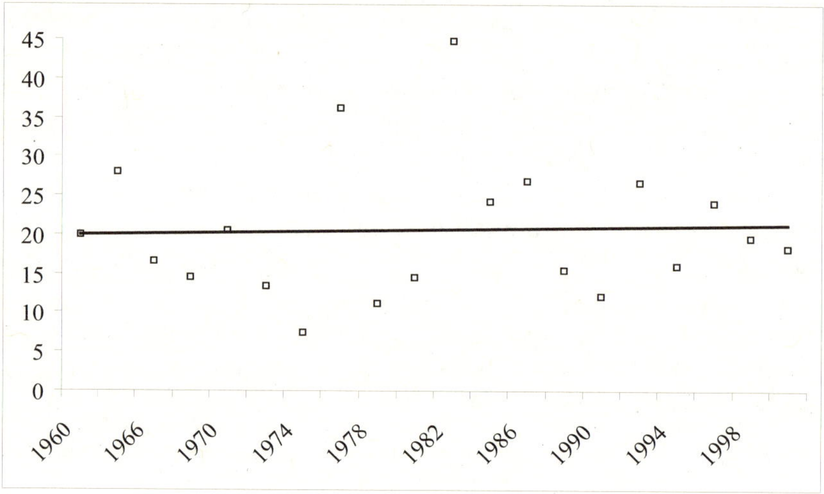

This finding is in fact less surprising than it seems, because the suggestion that an increasing salience of cultural issues undermines that of class issues relies on the debatable assumption that those two types of issues exhaust the full range of possibilities and therefore constitute a zero-sum game. This assumption is obviously naive, as there are many other types of problems that may be thought of as the most important ones facing the country (e.g., ecological problems, the quality of public transport, agricultural problems, etc.).

It is clear that cultural issues have become more salient since 1960 in the United States, but that the salience of class issues has not declined during this same period, in short. This brings us to our second question: whether and how issue salience affects the relationship between class and voting.

Class Voting, Cultural Voting, and Issue Salience

Class Voting and Cultural Voting

As we have argued earlier in this book, the major weakness of the received conceptualization of class voting—as measured by the Alford index and its statistically more advanced contemporary offshoots—resides in the assumption that class-based economic interests underlie the relationship between class and voting. This assumption is not so much plainly wrong, but rather one-sided. On the one hand, as we have seen, there is ample evidence that a weak class position does indeed lead to economic egalitarianism (see also Marshall et al. 1988: 179-183, Middendorp 1991, Scheepers et al. 1992, Weakliem and Heath 1994, Elchardus 1996, De Witte and Billiet 1999, Edlund 1999, Svallfors 1999) and that the latter does indeed encourage leftist voting (see also Weakliem and Heath 1994). On the other hand, however, the Alford index's striking omission of voting motivations obscures cross-cutting cultural voting that cross-pressures people to vote contrary to their class-based economic interests (see also Carmines and Layman 1997). Measuring the bivariate relationship between class and voting, the Alford index does thus not so much measure the level of class voting, but rather the degree to which the latter exceeds reversed cultural voting.

This means that class voting needs to be conceptualized and measured more explicitly as voting behavior that is guided by economic voting motivations (economic egalitarianism/conservatism) that are rooted in class-based economic interests, so as to be able to distinguish it from cultural voting, i.e., voting behavior that is guided by cultural voting motivations (authoritarianism/libertarianism) and that goes against class-based economic interests. This distinction between class voting and cultural voting reveals a classical cross-pressure mechanism (Lazarsfeld et al. 1972 [1944]: 53). Workers may vote either left on the basis of their economic egalitarianism (class voting) or right on the basis of their authoritarianism (cultural voting), just like members of the middle class may vote either right because of their economic conservatism (class voting) or left because of their libertarianism (cultural voting).

Using the conventional conception of class voting—the relationship between class and voting—as a baseline, the idea that class voting and cultural voting work in opposite directions informs two hypotheses. First, controlling for cultural voting, the baseline pattern is expected to shift in the direction of Alford's "natural and expected" pattern of a Republican-voting middle class and a Democratic-voting working class. Conversely, controlling for class voting, the baseline pattern is expected to shift away from Alford's "natural and expected" pattern in the direction of a Republican-voting working class and a Democratic-voting middle class.

The Role of Issue Salience

What exactly determines the strengths of class voting and cultural voting? In answering this question, Flanagan's (1979, 1982, 1987, Flanagan and Lee 2003) criticism of Inglehart's conceptualization and measurement of postmaterialism is highly relevant. Flanagan argues that Inglehart's index for postmaterialism collapses two logically unrelated phenomena: an authoritarianism/libertarianism value dimension on the one hand and the most salient type of political issues on the other. In the (most widely used) four-item version of Inglehart's index, Flanagan argues, the two goals that are taken to indicate "postmaterialism"—"Protecting freedom of speech" and "Giving the people more say in important political decisions"—are in fact indicators for libertarianism. The converse of this emphasis on individual liberty, according to Flanagan, is an authoritarian emphasis on "maintaining social order"—a political goal that Inglehart misconstrues as "materialism."

Whereas three of the four political goals used by Inglehart to distinguish "materialists" from "postmaterialists" tap into an authoritarian/libertarian dimension (Middendorp 1991: 262), it should come as no surprise that strong relationships have been reported between postmaterialism and authoritarianism/libertarianism (Steel et al. 1992, Dekker et al. 1999, Houtman 2003: 66-82). Moreover, Inglehart's misconstruction of "maintaining order in the nation" as indicating "materialism" rather than authoritarianism blocks out right-wing postmaterialists by definitional fiat. Flanagan therefore argues for the necessity to decompose Inglehart's index into an authoritarianism/libertarianism value dimension on the one hand and a distinction between "materialism" (salience of class issues) and "non-materialism" (salience of cultural issues) on the other.

Unlike the authoritarianism/libertarianism value dimension, the distinction between the two types of issue salience has no substantial ideological meaning and, because of that, it cannot influence the vote directly (Dekker et al., 1999; Flanagan, 1982). Those for whom materialist class issues are salient may be economically egalitarian or conservative, just like those for whom cultural issues are salient may have either libertarian or authoritarian value preferences (Flanagan 1987, Flanagan and Lee 2003). Issue salience is nevertheless important, Flanagan argues, because "an authoritarian-libertarian value preferences scale will tell us whether the respondent is likely to support the New Right or New Left issue agenda. A materialist-non-materialist value priorities scale will tell us whether the New Politics kinds of value concerns or the Old Politics economic issues will be foremost in the voter's mind when he or she makes a choice" (1987: 1306-1307). Although Flanagan does not provide empirical backup for this claim, other studies suggest that he is correct (Fournier et al. 2003, Layman and Carmines 1997).

The foregoing leads us to two additional hypotheses, that both relate to the role of issue salience in determining the strengths of class voting and cultural voting. We expect authoritarianism/libertarianism to more strongly affect the vote of those for whom cultural issues are salient and economic egalitarianism/conservatism that of those for whom class issues are salient.

Data and Measurement

We test our hypotheses with the *American National Election Studies* data for the 1996 and 2000 presidential elections, restricting our analysis to those respondents who are, on the one hand, employed for at least twenty hours a week, retired, or unemployed—so as to be able to meaningfully assign them a class position based on their (former) occupation—and who have, on the other hand, validly responded to the question about voting behavior during the latest presidential election (N=1,922). Hypotheses about the role of issue salience are tested with the random half of those respondents (N=976) to whom the relevant open-ended question has been administered. Indeed, we pool data for 1996 and 2000 to enable us to retain a sufficiently high number of respondents to test our hypotheses about whether or not issue salience conditions the degree to which economic egalitarianism/conservatism and authoritarianism/libertarianism affect the vote.

Issue salience has been measured as indicated above. Of the 976 respondents who responded to this question, 24 percent indicated that they were most concerned about a cultural problem, 20 percent that they were most concerned about a class problem and 56 percent that they considered any other problem most important.

Voting behavior is measured as the candidate voted for in the recent presidential elections. Of the 1,922 respondents, 53 percent voted for the Democratic presidential candidate and 47 percent for the Republican one (or for Perot in 1996).

Class is measured by means of a slightly revised version of the class schema devised by Manza and Brooks (1999: 57), that has some similarity to the EGP class schema used in Chapter 2.[5] It codes people into class positions on the basis of their current or last occupation and consists of five classes:

- Class I: *Professionals* (including lawyers, physicians, engineers, teachers, scientists, writers, editors, and social workers);
- Class II: *Managers and administrators* (including all non-retail sales managers);
- Class III: *Routine white-collar workers* (retail sales, clerical, and white collar service workers);
- Class IV: *Skilled manual workers and foremen* in all industries;
- Class V: *Semi and unskilled manual workers* in all industries (including farming and services).

We conceive of Classes I and II as middle class and Classes IV and V as working class, but again feel hesitant to qualify Class III as either, because whereas some emphasize the nonmanual character of routine white-collar occupations, qualifying them as middle class, others emphasize their routinized work situation, qualifying them as "white-collar proletarian"—and hence: working class (e.g., Wright 1979). Given this disagreement in the literature, we feel it is wiser to include them in neither.

Authoritarianism/libertarianism and *economic egalitarianism/conservatism* have been measured by means of six items about cultural issues such as the role of women, abortion, and moral decline[6] and seven items about economic issues such as government insurance of jobs and government spending on the poor and on welfare programs.[7] A factor analysis of these thirteen items yields the bi-dimensional structure that is typically found for those two types of values (e.g., Evans et al. 1996, Fleishman 1988, Heath et al. 1994, Middendorp 1991).[8] After reversing the items that require so, scale scores for authoritarianism/libertarianism are assigned to those with at least five valid scores on the relevant items. The same procedure is used to assign scale scores for economic egalitarianism/conservatism. High scores indicate libertarianism and economic conservatism, respectively.

Results

Because we are dealing with a binary dependent variable, we analyze the data by means of logistic regression analysis. Before testing our

Table 3.1
Voting Republican or Democrat Explained by Class
(1=Republican, 2=Democrat, log-odds ratios)

Independent variables	
Professionals (I)	-0.21
Managers and administrators (II)	-0.46***
Routine white-collar workers (III)	0.06
Skilled manual workers and foremen (IV)	-0.43
Semi and unskilled manual workers (V)[1]	0
Year 1996	0.05
Constant	0.34***
N	1,922
R^2 (Nagelkerke)	0.01

*p<0.05; **p<0.01; ***p<0.001
1. Reference category

hypotheses, we estimate the relationship between class position and voting behavior in the United States at the end of the twentieth century as our baseline model (see Table 3.1).[9]

The relationship between class and voting behavior proves embarrassingly weak. In fact, when it comes to voting, there is no difference at all between professionals (Class I) and semi and unskilled manual workers (Class V)—clearly two classes that differ widely in terms of key class-related characteristics such as income. Moreover, routine white-collar workers (Class III) and skilled manual workers and foremen (Class IV) do not set themselves apart by means of their voting from those two classes either: no voting differences exist between four of the five classes. Managers and administrators (Class II) are the only exception, then, being slightly more likely to vote for a Republican candidate than the four other classes. What should immediately be added to this, however, is that the size of this difference is in fact negligible. Variance explained does not even exceed 1 percent.

If anything, Table 3.1 underscores the relevance of the problem that we address in this book: isn't it very problematical, given those findings, that much research is still by and large driven by the assumption that a leftist-voting working class and a rightist-voting middle class constitutes the "natural and expected" pattern? This brings us to the question whether the virtual absence of a leftist-voting working class and a rightist-voting middle class is caused by cultural voting, that cross-pressures the working class to vote Republican and the middle class to vote Democratic. Table 3.2 points out that this is, indeed, the case. Once we cancel out cultural voting—the tendency to vote contrary to one's class interests, inspired by a cultural voting motivation—by statistically controlling for authoritarianism/libertarianism, the picture that emerges fits Alford's "natural and expected" pattern of class alignments a whole lot better.

The middle class has a clear tendency to vote Republican and the working class (including the routine white-collar workers of Class III) to vote Democratic. As expected, then, the conventional bivariate measurement of class voting criticized above does indeed make class voting invisible by mixing it up with reversed cultural voting. This confirms our hypothesis.

Now does the reverse apply, too? Does the baseline pattern shift further away from Alford's "natural and expected" pattern in the direction of a Republican-voting working class and a Democratic-voting middle class if we cancel out class voting, i.e., if we statistically control for economic egalitarianism/conservatism? It is clear that the baseline pattern does not change into one with a Democratic-voting middle class and a Republican-voting working class. But it is also clear that the sole finding that fitted the "natural and expected" pattern—i.e., the slight tendency of managers and administrators (Class II) to vote more Republican than the four other classes—disappears. Consistent with our expectations, then, controlling for class voting wipes out all electoral differences between the classes, making the baseline pattern shift even further away from Alford's "natural and expected" pattern. Those findings confirm that the bivariate relationship between class and voting, indeed, mixes up class voting and reversed cultural voting: controlling for one, the baseline pattern changes in the direction of that which is typical of the other type of voting.

This brings us to our final question, i.e., whether the type of issue deemed most important determines levels of class voting and cultural voting. Table 3.3 presents the relevant findings from three identical logistic regression models for the three different categories of issue salience that we distinguish.

Table 3.2
Voting Republican or Democrat Explained by Class, Economic Conservatism, and Libertarianism
(1=Republican, 2=Democrat, log-odds ratios)

Independent variables	Model 1	Model 2	Model 3
Professionals (I)	0.07	-0.41**	-0.12
Managers and administrators (II)	-0.10	-0.68***	-0.31
Routine white-collar workers (III)	0.26	0.06	0.23
Skilled manual workers and foremen (IV)	-0.25	-0.38	-0.19
Semi and unskilled manual workers (V)[1]	0	0	0
Economic conservatism	-1.63***		-1.48***
Libertarianism		1.39***	1.19***
Year 1996	0.27**	0.12	0.30**
Constant	0.43***	0.51***	0.55***
N	1,918	1,919	1,917
R^2 (Nagelkerke)	0.26	0.20	0.35

*$p<0.05$; **$p<0.01$; ***$p<0.001$
1. Reference category

Table 3.3
Voting Republican or Democrat Explained by Class, Economic Conservatism, and Libertarianism
(1=Republican, 2=Democrat, log-odds ratios)

Independent variables	Other issues	Class issues	Cultural issues
Professionals (I)	0.61	0.55	-1.07
Managers and administrators (II)	0.27	-0.55	-1.12
Routine white-collar workers (III)	-0.25	0.63	-0.31
Skilled manual workers and foremen (IV)	0.71	0.28	-0.18
Semi and unskilled manual workers (V)[1]	0	0	0
Economic conservatism	-1.34***	-1.69***	-1.32***
Libertarianism	0.99***	0.66	1.95***
Year 1996	0.27	0.35	0.53
Constant	0.30	0.43	0.23
N	555	195	233
R^2 (Nagelkerke)	0.28	0.35	0.46

*p<0.05; **p<0.01; ***p<0.001
1. Reference category

It is clear that cultural voting is strongest for those for whom cultural issues are salient. Among those, authoritarianism/libertarianism substantially more strongly drives the vote than in either of the two other categories of issue salience. Although libertarianism also increases the odds of voting Democratic rather than Republican among those with "other" types of issue salience, to be sure, it does so far more strongly if cultural issues are salient. Indeed, the relevant effect is significantly stronger among the latter category.[10] It is even more striking to note that cultural voting is completely absent if class issues are salient, i.e., if one feels that the most important problem facing the country relates to class inequality or economic distribution. Cultural voting is at its strongest, in short, if one feels that the most important problem facing the country is of a cultural or moral nature. Needless to say, this confirms our hypothesis.

Now does the reverse apply, too? Is class voting stronger among those for whom class issues are salient than for either of the two other categories of issue salience? Surprisingly, this is not the case. The degree to which economic egalitarianism/conservatism drives the vote is basically identical among those for whom class issues are salient, those for whom cultural issues are salient, and those for whom other types of issues are salient (there are no significant differences between the strengths of the effects).[11] This means that class voting is basically insensitive to issue salience: economic egalitarianism/conservatism drives the vote anyway, independent of the type of problem one considers most important.

Conclusion

We have found no evidence at all for a decline of class politics in this chapter. Not only have class issues retained their salience in the United States since 1960, but class voting moreover proves remarkably immune to shifts in issue salience: whether or not people vote according to their class-based economic interests does not depend on the type of issues that is salient. In this sense, one may say, class voting *is* a "natural" phenomenon. A leftist-voting working class and a rightist-voting middle class is certainly *not*, however. This is because bivariate relationships between class and voting do not actually measure class voting, but dilute it with cross-cutting cultural voting. As a consequence, the new consensus that Western countries have been witnessing a decline of class voting since World War II may be a mere artifact of the widespread application of the "Alford-index" and its statistically more sophisticated contemporary offshoots in political sociology since the 1960s.

Moving to cultural politics, it is clear from our findings that the salience of cultural issues has increased strongly since 1960 and it is also clear that cultural issue salience leads people to vote against their class-based economic interests. While salience of class issues does not strengthen the familiar pattern of a leftist-voting working class and a rightist-voting middle class, cultural issue salience *does* erode it—albeit not because it undermines class voting, but because it strengthens cultural voting. Our findings point out, then, that authoritarianism/libertarianism and cultural issue salience, the former driving votes contrary to class-based economic interests and the latter conditioning the strength of this tendency, need to be distinguished carefully in theorizing and empirical research. Inglehart's practice of lumping the two together in a single notion of "postmaterialism" obscures what is actually going on (see also Houtman 2003: 136-138).

The trends in issue salience among the American electorate that we have documented in this chapter raise the question whether cultural issues have become an increasingly important source of political conflict in the Western world generally. To answer this question, we study in Chapter 4 whether the trends in issue salience found among the American public since 1960 are also reflected in party manifestos in Western countries since World War II. We also study in Chapter 4 what those changing patterns of issue salience mean for the structure of political polarization. Have we been witnessing a decline of left and right since World War II, as many argue today, or rather a radical transformation of left and right, due to an increasing salience of cultural issues?

Notes

1. We are forced to exclude the *American National Election Studies* survey of 1962 and those administered prior to 1960, because these do not enable us to construct separate and adequate measures for the salience of both types of issues. This leaves us with a total of 29,280 respondents across the period 1960-2000.
2. The data collectors have coded answers to the aforementioned open-ended question and we have coded the following categories as indicating cultural issue salience: "pro-abortion," "anti-abortion," "women's rights," "moral/religious decay," "family problems," "problems with young people" (such as "sexual attitudes" or "lack of values/discipline"), "religion too mixed up in politics/school prayer" and "homosexuality" (see Layman and Carmines 1997: 765).
3. We have coded the following categories as indicating class issue salience: "minimum wage," "tax cuts," "class-oriented concerns," "distribution of wealth," "farm subsidies," "government control of sectors economy," "labor/union problems," "unemployment," "jobs," "social security," "poverty," and "social welfare."
4. Elections for presidency and for congress were included.

5. The Manza and Brooks class schema has two more categories than ours. First, due to lacking information on self-employment status, we could not code respondents into the class of "owners, proprietors, and other non-professional self-employed persons." Second, we chose not to code the "class" of "non-full-time labor-force participants," consisting of homemakers, retirees, students, and disabled working less than twenty hours a week, as this constitutes an extremely heterogeneous class, differing widely in terms of their relationship to the labor market. As explained above, retirees and the unemployed were coded into class positions based on their former occupations.

6. First, four Likert-type items with response categories 1, "Agree strongly," through 5, "Disagree strongly" have been used: "The newer lifestyles are contributing to the breakdown of our society!," "The world is always changing and we should adjust our view of moral behavior to those changes!," "This country would have many fewer problems if there were more emphasis on traditional family ties!," and "We should be more tolerant of people who choose to live according to their own moral standards, even if they are very different from our own!" Besides those four items, two questions with different (albeit ordinally ordered) response categories have been used: "Some people feel that women should have an equal role with men in running business, industry, and government. Others feel that a women's place is in the home. Where would you place yourself on this scale?" (response categories: 1, "Women and men should have an equal role," through 7, "Women's place is in the home") and "When should abortion be allowed by law?" (response categories: 1, "By law, abortion should never be permitted" through 4, "By law, a woman should always be able to obtain an abortion as a matter of personal choice"). Because of the different response formats, answers have been standardized before scale scores were assigned.

7. The first two are Likert-type items: "One of the big problems in this country is that we don't give everyone an equal chance!" and "It is not really that big a problem if some people have more of a chance in life than others!" (response categories: 1, "Agree strongly," through 5, "Disagree strongly"). Firstly, two questions on federal social spending have been added to those: "Should federal spending on poor people be increased, decreased or kept the same?" and "Should federal spending on welfare programs be increased, decreased or kept about the same?" (response categories: 1, "Increased," 2, "Same," and 3, "Decreased or cut out entirely"). Finally, three other questions about federal social spending have been added, all with seven response categories: "Some feel there should be a government insurance plan, which would cover all medical and hospital expenses for everyone. Others feel that all medical expenses should be paid by individuals, and through private insurance plans like Blue Cross or other company paid plans. Where would you place yourself on this scale?" (response categories: 1, "Government insurance plan," through 7, "Private insurance plan"); "Some people feel that the government in Washington should see to it that every person has a job and a good standard of living. Others think the government should just let each person get ahead on his/their own. Where would you place yourself on this scale?" (response categories: 1, "Government see to job and good standard of living," through 7, "Government let each person get ahead on his own"); "Some people think the government should provide fewer services, even in areas such as health and education, in order to reduce spending. Other people feel that it is important for the government to provide many more services even if it means an increase in spending. Where would you place yourself on this scale?" (response categories: 1, "Government should provide many fewer services: reduce spending a lot," through 7, "Government should provide many

more services: increase spending a lot"). As questions have unequal numbers of response categories, answers have been standardized before computing scale scores.
8. The correlation between the two scales is -0.27 (p<0.001), however, which is a lot stronger than typically found for two sets of items such as these.
9. Control variables have not been included in the model tested in Table 3.1, because supplementary analyses have pointed out that controlling for education, religion, region (political south versus non-south), gender, race and age does not yield substantially different results. Although the latter also applies to election year, we nevertheless feel it is proper to control for this, because we pool data from two different years.
10. We have tested for significance by combining the three subsamples of Table 3.3 into a single analysis, adding dummy variables for class and cultural issue salience as well as interaction terms of those dummies (coded 1 versus 2 for this purpose) with economic egalitarianism/conservatism and authoritarianism/libertarianism. The effect of the interaction term of cultural issue salience and authoritarianism/libertarianism proved significant, confirming that the latter affects the vote significantly more strongly among those for whom cultural issues are salient.
11. The relevant dummy variables referred to in the previous note had no significant effects.

4

The End of Left and Right?
The Transformation of Political Culture
(1945-1998)

Introduction

"The political landscape has changed. Right is no longer right, left no longer left." To this recent observation by Dutch politician Boris Dittrich[1] those of many others, including Bill Clinton and Tony Blair, can be added (Bobbio 1996). Traditionally, the struggle between left and right was a conflict over class issues, so that "in its classic connotation, molded by the traditional labor movement and by socialist parties, 'leftism' implied a commitment for stronger governmental control and intervention" (Geser 1998: 235). "Rightism" meant just the opposite: less state control of the economic system and, hence, less state-enforced economic redistribution.

Many believe today that this traditional distinction has lost much of its former appeal. It is felt that the major conflicts of the past, focusing on the distribution of scarce resources among society's classes, have by and large disappeared due to rising levels of affluence (Geser 1998, Inglehart 1997). Moreover, Sanders (1999: 182) notes, "the end of the cold war, and the attendant collapse of communism in eastern Europe, has robbed socialists worldwide of a viable working model of collectivism in action. For some observers on the left, Labour's shift to the right denied British voters a real ideological choice. The end of ideology which Daniel Bell had anticipated in the 1960s and which Francis Fukuyama had announced in 1990 had, perhaps, finally arrived" (see also: De Benoist 1995, Giddens 1994). Obviously, the decline of the familiar alignments of class and party only increases the credibility of accounts such as those. It is after all only a small step from noting that increasing numbers of people vote for the "wrong" parties to concluding that this process implies "the collapse of the left and right distinction" (Ignazi 2003: 6).

It is not clear at all whether differences between left and right are simply disappearing, however, and it is in fact more typically argued that political polarization is changing (Abrahamson and Inglehart 1995, Flanagan 1987, Ignazi 2003, Inglehart 1987, Kitschelt and Hellemans 1990, Knutsen 1998). In this view, polarization over "old" issues of class decreases, while simultaneously polarization over "new" cultural issues increases, with the left thus increasingly pushing libertarian agendas and the right authoritarian ones. In the words of Knutsen (1998: 65): "In advanced industrial society, "New Politics" have become a significant line of conflict, and new parties and party families have polarized the party system along a new line of conflict. This new line has been conceptualized somewhat differently by different authors: as materialist/post-materialist, libertarian/authoritarian, or left-libertarian versus right-authoritarian."

Because we need to study changes in issue salience before we can address these alleged changes in political polarization, we start with the former in order to see whether what we found in Chapter 3 for American voters also applies to postwar manifestos of political parties in western countries generally. Have cultural issues become more salient in this case, too? If so, what has happened to the old issues of class? Have they retained their salience in those manifestos as well?

Again: From Class Issues to Cultural Issues?

Data

We rely on the Party Manifesto Data (Budge et al. 2001) to determine changes in the political cultures of Western countries in the postwar era (1945-1998). From those data, analyzed by Clark (2001b) for similar purposes, we select only the twenty countries that were previously studied by Nieuwbeerta. Each sentence and quasi-sentence has been coded into one of 56 policy priorities. The data are structured in such a way that, for each party manifesto, all sentences and quasi-sentences amount to 100 percent, with all sentences pertaining to a particular policy priority expressed as a percentage of the whole. A score on a policy priority thus reflects the space this priority occupies in the party manifesto. We have weighted the data by the share of the vote won by the parties to bring the influence of small (often extremist) parties on the mean scores obtained for countries and years back to proper proportions.[2]

Changing Issue Salience?

Measuring the salience of four types of issues separately (leftist and rightist class issues and authoritarian and libertarian cultural ones), we take the one-dimensional left-right scale devised by Budge and Klingemann (2001) as our point of departure (see also Budge et al. 1987). This scale is intended to measure the positions of political parties on a one-dimensional left-right continuum and hence comprises both class issues and cultural issues. To be able to distinguish those, and to make a further left-right distinction within each of them, we add a number of issues so as to arrive at equal numbers for each of the four indices we want to construct (see Table 4.1).[3] In all instances, higher scores indicate higher levels of issue salience.

Table 4.1
Construction of Four Indices for Issue Salience

Rightist class issues	Leftist class issues
Free enterprise*	Controlled economy*
Economic incentives*	Economic planning*
Economic orthodoxy*	Nationalization*
Welfare state limitation*	Welfare state expansion*
Authoritarian cultural issues	*Libertarian cultural issues*
National way of life positive*	National way of life negative
Traditional morality positive*	Traditional morality negative
Law and order*	Underprivileged minority groups

* Issues also included in the Budge and Klingemann left-right scale.

How has the salience of authoritarian and libertarian cultural issues and that of rightist and leftist class issues developed in the postwar period in Western societies? Table 4.2 presents the correlations between election year and the four indices for issue salience.

It is clear that cultural issue salience has increased strongly. Although libertarian cultural issues have lost much of their salience in Finland, they have become significantly more salient in six other countries: Canada, Denmark, Germany, Ireland, the Netherlands, and Switzerland. The same applies to authoritarian issues: while their salience has declined in Luxembourg, it has increased significantly in no less than eight other countries. Examples are Australia, Denmark, Ireland, and the United States.

This increasing salience of cultural issues does not mean that class issues have become less salient, however. Although leftist class issues have become less salient in five countries, their salience has increased in two others (i.e., Greece and Portugal). Moreover, the salience of rightist class issues has declined in none of those twenty countries and even increased strongly in four of them. It is clear, then, that we again cannot conclude that the salience of class issues has collapsed. Although the salience of leftist class issues has declined, that of rightist ones has only increased since World War II.

Finally, we collapse the upper eight items in Table 4.1 into a single index for the salience of class issues and the lower eight into one for cultural issue salience. Table 4.3 points out that we find three positive and three negative trends for the salience of class issues, showing a remarkable balance in the number of countries in which they have become more and less salient. The picture is strikingly different for cultural issues. We find strong and positive trends in no less than nine countries (United States, Sweden, Ireland, Italy, Great Britain, Germany, Denmark, Canada, and Australia) and in only two countries (Spain and Belgium) have cultural issues become less salient. Figure 4.1 summarizes the trend of the salience of both types of issues since World War II.

Based on this evidence, we reject two notions that lie at the heart of the work of Inglehart and others about the change of political culture (e.g., Clark 2001b). First, our findings contradict the notion that if cultural issues have become more salient, then surely that of class issues must have declined. We find no evidence for such a decline. Even though the salience of leftist class issues has declined, that of rightist ones has increased, so that we find no evidence for a clear overall trend for class issues. Like in the previous chapter, then, we conclude that class issues have not become less salient.

Table 4.2
Trends for Leftist and Rightist Class Issue Salience and Libertarian and Authoritarian Cultural Issue Salience, 1945-1998 (Pearson's r, two-tailed test)

Country	N	Leftist class issues	Rightist class issues	Libertarian issues	Authoritarian issues
Australia	22	0.00	0.19	0.41	0.65***
Austria	15	-0.36	0.05	0.46	-0.25
Belgium	17	-0.31	0.01	-0.26	-0.17
Canada	17	-0.49*	0.17	0.81***	0.61**
Denmark	21	0.24	0.30	0.48*	0.83***
Finland	15	0.43	0.14	-0.65**	-0.08
France	14	0.46	0.72**	0.05	0.15
Germany	14	-0.74**	-0.16	0.81***	0.58*
Great Britain	14	-0.54*	-0.38	-0.08	0.79**
Greece	8	0.70*	0.59	-0.05	-0.44
Ireland	15	0.08	0.48	0.57*	0.58*
Italy	14	-0.15	0.77**	0.43	0.47
Luxembourg	12	0.07	0.82**	0.49	-0.58*
The Netherlands	16	-0.46	-0.37	0.88***	-0.44
Norway	14	-0.56*	0.57*	0.33	0.06
Portugal	9	0.71*	0.17	-0.09	0.05
Spain	7	0.26	-0.31	-0.05	-0.63
Sweden	17	-0.65**	0.08	0.39	0.70**
Switzerland	13	0.16	-0.28	0.79**	0.08
United States	13	0.30	0.21	-0.07	0.76**
Total	287	-0.14*	0.12*	0.24***	0.19***

*p<0.05; **p<0.01; ***p<0.001

Table 4.3
Trends for Class Issue Salience and Cultural Issue Salience, 1945-1998
(Pearson's r, two-tailed test)

Country	N	Class issue salience	Cultural issue salience
Australia	22	0.19	0.67**
Austria	15	-0.13	-0.10
Belgium	17	-0.22	-0.33
Canada	17	-0.31	0.75**
Denmark	21	0.42	0.81***
Finland	15	0.47	-0.37
France	14	0.76**	0.19
Germany	14	-0.78**	0.69**
Great Britain	14	-0.12	0.75**
Greece	8	0.71*	-0.43
Ireland	15	0.06	0.63**
Italy	14	0.69**	0.56*
Luxembourg	12	0.45	-0.50
The Netherlands	16	-0.54*	-0.14
Norway	14	-0.07	0.30
Portugal	9	0.56	0.00
Spain	7	0.11	-0.72
Sweden	17	-0.52*	0.66**
Switzerland	13	-0.07	0.32
United States	13	0.30	0.76**

*p<0.05; **p<0.01; ***p<0.001

Our findings also contradict Inglehart's notion that left-libertarian issues ("postmaterialism') have become more salient and right-authoritarian ones ("materialism') less so. Although, consistent with his theory, libertarian issues have become more salient in the postwar period, the same applies to authoritarian ones that stress the importance of traditional morality and law and order. Our findings thus point out that Inglehart's index for postmaterialism is not particularly useful for mapping changes in the political culture. Given the simultaneous increase of libertarian and authoritarian cultural issues, it is after all not a very good idea to subsume the former under the label of "postmaterialism" and the latter under that of "materialism" and then proceed to measure postmaterialism in such a way that the two become mutually exclusive.

Whither Political Polarization?

Measuring Political Polarization

Most studies that address the question whether we have been witnessing a convergence of left and right preclude the theoretically vital possibility that cultural polarization has gradually replaced class polarization beforehand. This is because, like in the Budge and Klingemann scale referred to above, class issues and cultural issues are typically lumped

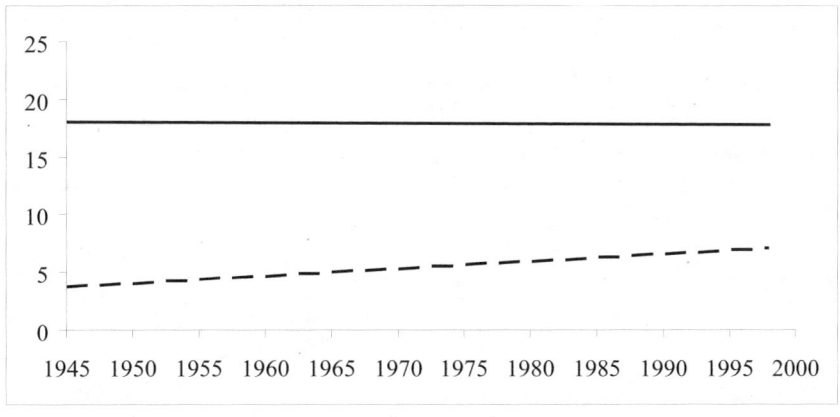

Figure 4.1
Trends for Class Issue Salience and Cultural Issue Salience, 1945-1997
(linear regression trend lines, N=291)

—— Salience of class issues (Pearson's r=-0.01, n.s.)

— — — Salience of cultural issues (Pearson's r=0.28, p<0.001)

together rather than systematically distinguished. The reader is referred to Achterberg (2006: 43-45) for a critical discussion of this and other shortcomings in the most widely used strategies of addressing the question of a convergence of left and right. Remarkable as it may seem, we do not know a single study that has systematically addressed the question whether polarization over class issues has decreased over the years and has been replaced by polarization over cultural issues.

Yet, there is some research literature about whether polarization over cultural issues has increased over the years and whether general polarization between left and right has declined. Contrary to the suggestion in the American *Culture Wars* debate that polarization over cultural issues increases (Hunter 1991), no such trend has been found for the American electorate (DiMaggio et al. 1996). It is not even clear whether polarization over abortion—clearly one of the decisive cultural issues in the American context—has increased (Evans and Bryson 2001, Mouw and Sobel 2001). Research among European electorates has yielded roughly the same conclusion: no clear trends in polarization over cultural issues are found (Draulans and Halman 2003). Although all of those studies thus deny that polarization over cultural issues has increased, it is quite problematic that they all rely on trends over twenty years at a maximum, which may be far too short (Budge 2000), especially considering the vital influence of the 1960s counterculture.

The data analyzed in this chapter, ranging all the way back to World War II, allow for a more satisfactory analysis. We first construct a scale that indicates the extent to which party manifestos emphasize rightist or leftist class issues and a scale that indicates the degree to which they emphasize authoritarian or libertarian cultural ones. For the former, the number of endorsed leftist class issues is subtracted from the number of endorsed rightist ones; for the latter, the same is done with authoritarian and libertarian ones. This yields two indices with high scores indicating an emphasis on rightist class issues and authoritarian cultural issues, respectively.

The two newly constructed scales are sufficiently valid and reliable. When we combine both scales into a single one-dimensional left-right scale, this combined scale correlates no less than 0.86 (p<0.001) with the Budge and Klingemann scale that has in the meantime proven to be valid and reliable. Moreover, correlations for five different periods between our two indices and the Budge and Klingemann scale point out that they both tap into the left-right dimension as measured by the latter (see Table 4.4).[4]

Table 4.4
Relationships Between the Budge and Klingemann Left-Right Scale, the Class Left-Right Scale, and the Libertarian-Authoritarian Scale
(Pearson's r, two-tailed test)

Year	N	Class left-right scale and Budge and Klingemann left-right scale	Libertarian-authoritarian scale and Budge and Klingemann left-right scale
1945-1955	277	0.75***	0.36***
1956-1965	256	0.79***	0.28***
1966-1975	325	0.73***	0.44***
1976-1985	391	0.80***	0.44***
1986-1998	459	0.80***	0.50***

***$p<0.001$

Based on the left-right and authoritarian-libertarian indices, we next construct measures for polarization by calculating standard deviations of the positions of political parties during elections in particular countries and years. The higher these standard deviations for a particular combination of country and year, the larger the differences between the relevant parties—and hence, the more polarization. Reversely: the more identical the parties, the lower the standard deviation, and the weaker the polarization. Higher scores, in short, indicate more party polarization.

Results

Table 4.5 shows the development of both types of polarization since World War II for the twenty countries separately. Polarization over class issues has increased only in France, while it has decreased in four other countries (Australia, Belgium, the Netherlands, and Sweden). Cultural polarization has declined in Spain, Portugal, and the Netherlands, and increased in no less than seven countries (Australia, Canada, Denmark, France, Great Britain, Sweden, and Switzerland).

Those trends of political polarization are consistent with the idea that the meaning of left and right has changed over the years: polarization over class issues has declined and has increasingly given way to polarization over cultural issues. This is visualized in Figure 4.2 for all countries together.

Figure 4.2
Trends for Polarization over Class Issues and Cultural Issues, 1945-1997 (linear regression trend lines, N=291)

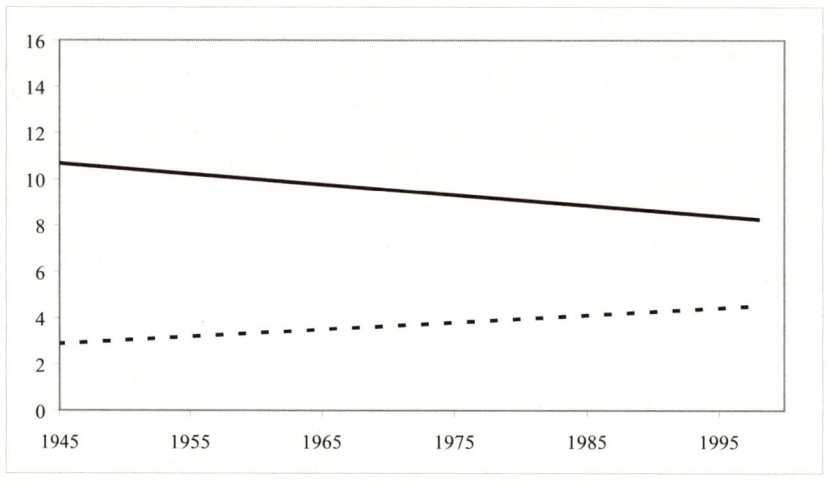

———— Polarization over class issues (Pearson's r=-0.17; p<0.01)

— — — — Polarization over cultural issues (Pearson's r=0.19; p<0.001)

Although this is not visible in Figure 4.2, cultural polarization was remarkably strong in the first five years immediately after World War II (probably due to the war itself) and a whole lot weaker in the early 1950s. This high level of cultural polarization in this brief postwar period pushes down the upward trend of cultural issue polarization substantially. In fact, when we control for this phenomenon, the trend becomes stronger and Pearson's r increases from 0.19 to 0.23.

Shifting Parties and Changing Polarization

Are the observed changes in polarization due to ideological shifts by particular party families that may be distinguished?[5] Do they mean, for instance, that parties on the left have become more libertarian and parties on the right more authoritarian on cultural issues? And what has happened with the stance of leftist and rightist parties when it comes to class issues? Table 4.6 shows the trends for the mean position on the authoritarianism-libertarianism index for cultural issues and the left-right index for class issues.

Table 4.5
Trends for Polarization over Class Issues and Cultural Issues, 1945-1997
(Pearson's r, two-tailed test)

Country	N	Class left-right scale	Cultural left-right scale
Australia	22	-0.44*	0.48*
Austria	15	-0.04	0.27
Belgium	17	-0.54*	-0.31
Canada	17	-0.30	0.68**
Denmark	21	0.27	0.66**
Finland	15	0.04	0.55*
France	14	0.62*	0.41
Germany	14	-0.19	0.57*
Great Britain	14	-0.21	0.44
Greece	8	0.38	-0.28
Ireland	15	-0.30	-0.26
Italy	14	-0.02	0.32
Luxembourg	12	0.27	-0.56
The Netherlands	16	-0.52*	-0.73**
Norway	14	0.36	-0.59*
Portugal	9	0.08	-0.35
Spain	7	0.12	-0.89**
Sweden	17	-0.60*	0.53*
Switzerland	13	0.52	0.73**
United States	13	-0.02	0.02

*p<0.05; **p<0.01

Table 4.6
Trends for Class Left-Right and Cultural Libertarian-Authoritarian Positions for Ten Party Families, 1945-1997
(Pearson's r, two-tailed test)

Party family	Class left-right	Cultural libertarianism-authoritarianism	N
Ecological	0.24	-0.21	45
Former Communist	-0.05	-0.10	182
Social Democratic	0.32**	-0.05	359
Liberal	0.07	0.03	222
Christian Democratic/religious	-0.07	-0.07	198
Conservative	0.01	0.25**	247
Nationalist	0.63**	0.29	45
Agrarian	-0.15	0.09	101
Ethnic and regional	0.07	0.10	42
Special interest	0.22	0.24*	68
Left (first three combined)	0.21**	-0.09*	586
Non-left (rest combined)	0.01	0.07*	923

*p<0.05; **p<0.01

In spite of the shift of communist parties in the opposite direction, leftist parties generally turn out to have shifted to the right when it comes to class issues. Leftist parties have furthermore shifted somewhat towards the libertarian end of the scale when it comes to cultural issues. Christian parties have moved to the left on both types of issues, while liberal parties show remarkable stability across time in both respects. Conservative parties have remained stable when it comes to class issues, but have moved strongly to the authoritarian end of the cultural scale.

All in all, as shown at the bottom of Table 4.6, especially leftist parties have changed their positions: they have become more rightist on class issues and more libertarian on cultural ones. Trends are weaker and non-significant for non-leftist parties. Decreased polarization over

Figure 4.3
Trend for Polarization over Class Issues by Trend for Class Issue Salience, 1945-1997 (Pearson's r=0.74, p<0.05, one-tailed test)

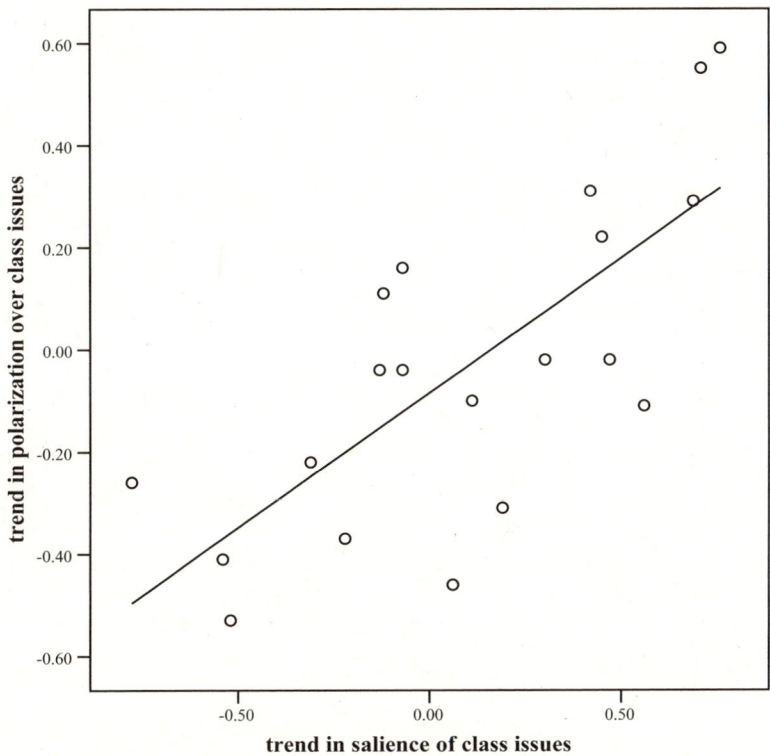

class issues is thus mainly due to a rightist shift of leftist parties, while increased polarization over cultural issues is due to both a libertarian shift of the latter and an authoritarian shift of rightist parties.

The final question that must be answered is whether polarization over a particular type of issues increases when its salience increases (and *vice versa*). Figure 4.3 shows that in countries in which class issues have become more salient (e.g., France, Denmark, and Portugal), polarization over these issues has also increased, while in countries in which the former has declined (e.g., the Netherlands, Sweden, and Germany), the latter has done so, too.

The same applies to cultural issues, as Figure 4.4 demonstrates, although the relationship is somewhat weaker in this case. In countries in which cultural issues have become more salient in the postwar period

Figure 4.4
Trend for Polarization over Cultural Issues by Trend for Cultural Issue Salience, 1945-1997 (Pearson's r=0.57, p<0.05, one-tailed test)

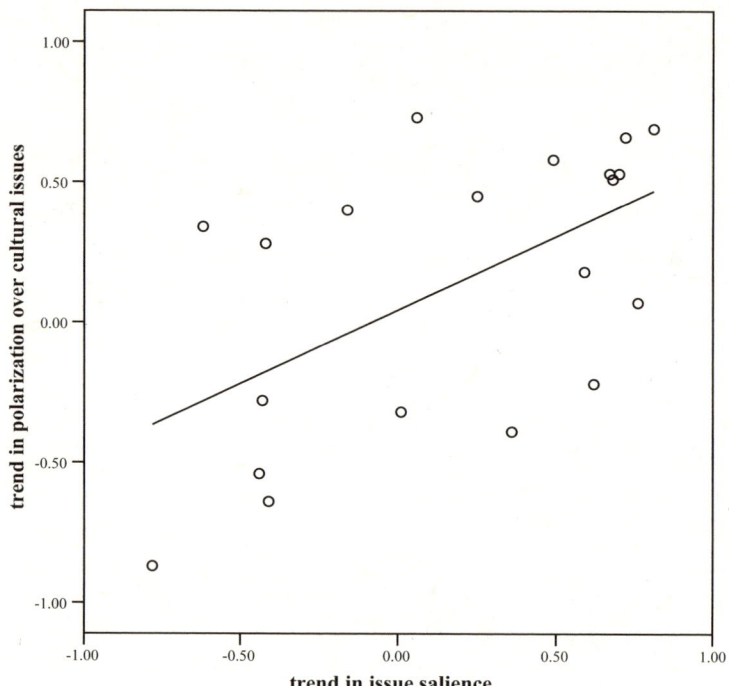

(e.g., United States, Canada, Denmark, and Germany), polarization over these issues has also increased. In countries in which the salience of those issues has declined (such as Spain, the Netherlands, and Luxembourg), polarization over those issues has also declined.

Conclusion

Our findings leave little to the imagination. It is clear that there has been a shift from a political culture that revolves around class issues towards one in which cultural issues are central. This does not mean that class issues have become less salient, however. Just like we found for the American electorate since the 1960s in Chapter 3, we now also find for political parties in the Western world generally that the salience of class issues has remained remarkably stable since World War II. Although polarization over those issues has declined, they are as salient as ever and polarization over them has certainly not disappeared.

Those are remarkable findings—not so much because they contradict those of other studies, but because they contradict today's virtual consensus that class politics is on the wane (e.g., Clark and Lipset 2001, Pakulski and Waters 1996, Hechter 2004). This consensus is hardly based on solid empirical evidence and we know of no systematically conducted internationally comparative study that demonstrates convincingly that the "old" politics of class has declined. Although studies into changing patterns of voting such as the one by Nieuwbeerta (1995, 1996, 2001, Nieuwbeerta and De Graaf 1999) are often interpreted as such, there is ample reason for skepticism, because these studies not only mix up class voting and cultural voting, but fail to study changes in issue salience in a more direct fashion, too.

As we have seen, there is no doubt that cultural issues have become more salient in the postwar period. It is also clear that party polarization over class issues has increasingly been giving way to polarization over cultural issues. Indeed, the coming of the new political culture takes shape in increasing salience of cultural issues as well as increasing party polarization over these. It is important to emphasize that the latter development strictly speaking cannot even be reconciled with Inglehart's claim that "new" cultural politics is basically left-libertarian. How, after all, could an increasing polarization over cultural issues take place if the salience of right-authoritarian issues would not have increased in tandem with that of left-libertarian ones?

It is unmistakably true that cultural politics has increased strongly, in short, but there is not much evidence that this has gone at the cost of class politics. Indeed, our findings so far suggest a new solution to the intriguing theoretical puzzle raised by Nieuwbeerta's work. On the one hand, his work has been decisive in demonstrating that the relationship between class and voting behavior has declined in most Western countries since World War II (Nieuwbeerta 1995, 1996, 2001, Nieuwbeerta and De Graaf 1999). On the other hand, his attempt to explain this downward trend fails, and our findings so far suggest that this is because his reliance on class theory leads him to theorize about contexts that are assumed to affect the salience of class issues (Nieuwbeerta 1995: 57-77, Nieuwbeerta and Ultee 1999). Our findings in this chapter, however, suggest that the erosion of the familiar alignment of the working class with the left and the middle class with the right has not so much been caused by a decline of class voting, but rather by an increase of cultural voting. Whether such is actually the case is the question that we will address in Chapter 5.

Notes

1. See: http://www.borisdittrich.nl/article.php?sid=190; last visited 23 March 2005 (our own translation from Dutch).
2. This weighting procedure does not prove to affect our findings in any significant way though.
3. The exact issues used in the scales and a short description of the items can be found in Appendix 1.
4. Table 4.4 also demonstrates that the relationships between the Budge and Klingemann scale and our index for the strength of the emphasis on authoritarian rather than libertarian cultural issues has become stronger as time has passed by. This indicates that cultural issues have increasingly come into the center of the left-right distinction.
5. Parties included in the data were coded into party families.

5

A Decline of Class Voting?
Class Voting and Cultural Voting in the Postwar Era (1956-1990)

With Jeroen van der Waal

Introduction

Our findings so far suggest that the newly grown consensus to the effect that class voting has declined since World War II was built on quicksand. Nieuwbeerta (1995, 1996, 2001, Nieuwbeerta and De Graaf 1999) may well have demonstrated that the relationship between class and voting has declined in the postwar era, but it remains to be seen whether this really means that class voting has declined. Besides our own findings in the previous chapters, there are a number of others that suggest otherwise.

Stonecash (2000) feels that the available empirical evidence cannot carry the weight of the new consensus. Relying on income as a less ambiguous and hence more valid class measure than Nieuwbeerta does, he has demonstrated that class voting has in fact become stronger in the United States since World War II. He argues that Inglehart's studies into the expansion of postmaterialism and cultural politics have wrongly been taken to imply a decline in class politics: "To ask a series of questions that do not ask about material conflicts, and then use the results to argue that material concerns are declining is surely one of the oddest logics of analysis ever presented in social science" (Stonecash 2000: 152).

We have not only found, consistent with Stonecash's findings, that the salience of class issues has not declined since World War II, but also that the latter does not even affect the strength of the relationship between class and voting. Moreover, as we have already pointed out—and also suggesting that something is seriously wrong with the newly grown consensus—contextual hypotheses derived from the class theory of politics prove strikingly impotent in explaining the strength of the relationship between class and voting (Nieuwbeerta 1995, Nieuwbeerta and Ultee 1999).

Taken together, those findings suggest that the erosion of the traditional alignment of the working class with the left and the middle class with the right since World War II has been caused by an increase of cultural voting rather than a decline of class voting. In this chapter, we study whether such is indeed the case. We do so by means of a re-analysis of Nieuwbeerta's data, on which much of the newly grown intellectual consensus in political sociology is based.

Disentangling Class Voting and Cultural Voting

Class Voting and Cultural Voting

Chapter 2 points out that education cannot be taken to indicate class just like income does, although sociologists have always underscored that those two variables are basically two of a kind, be it referred to as class or as socio-economic status (e.g., Duncan 1961, Hout et al. 1993, Ishida and Muller 1995, Kohn 1977 [1969], Kohn and Slomczynski 1990, Lipset 1981, Marshall et al. 1988, Van de Werfhorst and De Graaf 2004). As we have seen, education can be considered a class indicator if the explanation of economic egalitarianism is at stake, but it cannot when we are dealing with authoritarianism/libertarianism (see also Houtman 2001, 2003).

Because occupation-based class measures are inevitably strongly related to income as well as education (and, hence, to both economic egalitarianism/conservatism and authoritarianism/libertarianism), the Alford index inevitably mixes up *class voting*, i.e., voting for a leftist (rightist) party on the basis of economic egalitarianism (conservatism) that is rooted in a weak (strong) class position, with *cultural voting*, i.e., voting for a rightist (leftist) party on the basis of authoritarianism (libertarianism) that is rooted in a low (high) level of education. As we have seen, the latter has nothing to do with the former, because it is driven by a cultural rather than an economic voting motivation, stems from education rather than class, and cross-pressures the electorate to vote contradictory to its class-based economic interests.

Figure 5.1 disentangles both types of voting: the upper part denotes class voting and the lower part cross-cutting cultural voting. It points out that the strength of the relationship between class and voting, as measured by the Alford index, cannot tell us anything about the degree to

Figure 5.1
Class Voting Distinguished from Cultural Voting

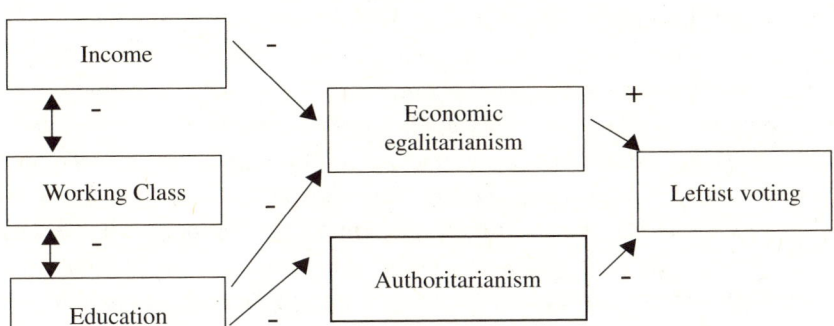

which class affects the vote. This is because both types of voting work in opposite directions and may vary independent of one another. A preference for economic redistribution that is rooted in a weak class position and that drives leftist voting, perfectly consistent with the logic of class voting, can thus be made invisible by an equally strong tendency among the poorly educated to vote for rightist parties, driven by high levels of authoritarianism. Measuring class voting as the strength of the bivariate relationship between class and voting then leads to the mistaken conclusion that "class does not affect the vote." Chapters 2 and 3 point out that this is not merely a hypothetical construction, but rather a realistic image of what occurs in the real world (see also Houtman 2001, 2003: 103-120). Reliance on the bivariate relationship between class and voting can even produce the conclusion that "class voting has declined" if it has in fact increased. This happens if class voting and cultural voting have both increased, but the latter more so than the former.

Hypotheses

It is not clear at all, to sum up the foregoing, whether the decline of the familiar alignment of the working class with the left and the middle class with the right since World War II, convincingly documented by Nieuwbeerta (1995, 1996, 2001, Nieuwbeerta and De Graaf 1999), has really been caused by a decline of class voting. It is certainly possible that it has, but it may also have been caused by an increase of cultural voting. Indeed, as we have already briefly indicated, three sets of findings point in the direction of the latter possibility.

Firstly, Stonecash (2000: 140), relying on income for the measurement of class, has demonstrated that the relationship between class and voting has become stronger rather than weaker in the United States since World War II, concluding: "rather than class divisions fading in relevance, they are likely to be a staple of American politics for some time." Telling detail: Nieuwbeerta relies on the same data as Stonecash, although he adds data from other countries to those. The difference between their findings, then, seems particularly caused by Stonecash's decision to use income categories and Nieuwbeerta's to instead rely on the (occupation-based) EGP class schema. Our discussion so far points out that this is not a trivial difference, because income categories, unlike occupational categories, are not susceptible to the problem of mixing up class voting and cultural voting, because no relationship exists between income and authoritarianism/libertarianism. With those two operationalizations of class producing such radically different findings, the decline of the traditional class-party alignments found by Nieuwbeerta more likely denotes an increase of cultural voting than a decline of class voting.

Secondly, if a decline of class voting had taken place since World War II, we would expect that class issues would have become less politically salient during this period. This is not the case however, as we have seen in the preceding chapters, although it is abundantly clear that cultural issues of individual liberty and social order have become much more salient during this period (see also Layman 2001, Hechter 2004). Moreover, it is striking that the salience of class issues does not affect the strength of the relationship between class and voting at all, whereas this relationship is substantially weaker if cultural issues are more salient, as we have seen (Chapter 3). This suggests, again, that we have not been witnessing a decline of class voting, but rather an increase of cultural voting since World War II.

Thirdly, and we have referred to this earlier, class analysis proves remarkably impotent in predicting the periods and countries in which the relationship between class and voting is weakest. Hypotheses derived from the class theory of politics, predicting the circumstances under which class distinctions are more or less salient, are rejected almost without exception (Nieuwbeerta 1995, Nieuwbeerta and Ultee 1999). If differences in the bivariate relationship between class and voting are taken to indicate differences in levels of class voting, those findings are obviously very surprising. Although it is of course conceivable that the class theory of politics is completely flawed, we consider it more likely that differences in the bivariate relationship between class and voting do actually not so much indicate differences in class voting, but rather differences in cultural voting. If such is the case, as suggested by the two other clusters of findings that we have just discussed, the failure of hypotheses derived from the class theory of politics ceases to be surprising. This theory, after all, obviously cannot explain the strength of cultural voting.

To find out whether the declining alignment of the working class with the left and the middle class with the right has been caused by a decline of class voting or by an increase of cultural voting, we test two hypotheses by means of a re-analysis of Nieuwbeerta's data. The first one tests whether a decline of class voting has occurred. It predicts that the decline of the relationship between EGP class and voting behavior has been caused by a decline of the tendency of those with low incomes to vote for parties on the left and those with high incomes to vote for parties on the right. The second hypothesis tests whether an increase of cultural voting has taken place. It predicts that the decline of the relationship between EGP class and voting behavior has been caused by an increase of the tendency of the poorly educated to vote for parties on the right and the highly educated to vote for parties on the left.

Data and Measurement

Data

As mentioned above, we re-analyze the data Nieuwbeerta has used to demonstrate the decline of the traditional alignment of the working class with the left and the middle class with the right (Nieuwbeerta and Ganzeboom 1996). Due to two deviations from Nieuwbeerta's measurement of voting behavior, to be discussed below, we restrict our analysis to data about 93,567 respondents, who have been sampled in 15 different countries between 1956 and 1990, adding up to a total of 80 combinations of country and year (see Table 5.1).

Measurement

Like Nieuwbeerta, we use the *EGP class schema*. As explained in Chapter 2, it is somewhat difficult to classify Classes III and V as unambiguously working class or middle class. In interpreting the statistical results, then, especially the voting behavior of the higher professionals (Class I), lower professionals (Class II), and petty bourgeoisie (Class IV) on the one hand ("middle class") and the skilled (Class VI) and semi and unskilled manual workers (Class VII) on the other ("working class") is important. EGP class is entered into the analysis as a series of six dummy variables, using the higher professionals (Class I) as the reference category.

Table 5.1
Number of Data Files for Each of the Combinations of Country and Period (1956-1990, N=80)

Country	1956-1970	1971-1980	1981-1990	Total	Period
Australia	1	-	3	4	1985-1987
Austria	-	1	3	4	1974-1989
Belgium	-	1	-	1	1975
Canada	-	-	1	1	1984
Denmark	-	1	-	1	1972
Finland	-	2	-	2	1972-1975
France	-	1	-	1	1978
Germany	1	2	6	9	1969-1990
Great Britain	-	2	6	8	1974-1990
Ireland	-	-	1	1	1990
Italy	1	1	-	2	1968-1975
The Netherlands	1	6	7	14	1970-1990
Norway	1	2	4	7	1965-1990
Switzerland	-	1	-	1	1976
United States	7	8	9	24	1956-1990
Total	12	28	40	80	1956-1990

Following Erikson (1984), net household *income* is used to determine income levels. Because people are likely to evaluate their income levels relative to national averages, income has first been standardized for each country and year combination separately. To allow for a comparison of the regression coefficients for income with these of the other independent variables, we have next applied a second standardization across all countries and years.

To standardize the educational classifications in the 15 countries, *education* has first been recoded into the number of years minimally required to attain the level of education at hand and has next been standardized by means of the same two-step procedure as income.

Like Nieuwbeerta (1995: 35), we use three different measures of *voting behavior*: the party one would vote for if elections were held today (or soon), the party one has voted for in the past, and the party one identifies with. If valid answers to all of these three questions are available, we use the first one, i.e., voting intention. If valid answers to only the last two are available, we use party identification. We do not use Nieuwbeerta's crude left versus non-left distinction, because it inevitably creates more or less arbitrary decisions in coding parties in the political center. We instead assign left-right scores to all political parties according to the left-right self-placement of those who vote for them, thus constructing a continuous variable with high scores indicating rightist voting.[1] It is quite remarkable, for that matter, that Nieuwbeerta codes new-leftist parties as non-leftist parties. Given massive support for those parties from the middle class (Hoffman-Martinot 1991, Inglehart 1997: 273-288), it needs no further argument that this decision produces a less dramatic decline of the relationship between class and voting than has actually occurred.

Results

Before testing our two hypotheses, we demonstrate that EGP class, education, and income are related in ways that make EGP class too ambiguous a variable in the study of class voting. We apply multilevel regression analysis, conceiving of country, year, and respondent as three different levels of analysis.

Table 5.2 points out that substantial income differences exist between the seven EGP classes (Model 1). The class of higher professionals has the highest average income and the classes of skilled, semi and unskilled manual workers the lowest. The classes also differ strongly with respect to education, however, and this accounts for a substantial part of those income differences (Model 2). The seven classes differ strongly with respect to both income and education, in short, and this makes EGP class too ambiguous a variable for the study of class voting. Whereas income and education both drive class voting, as we have argued above, it is after all education alone that constitutes the driving force behind cross-cutting cultural voting.

This decline of the relationship between EGP class and voting behavior cannot be interpreted as indicating a decline of class voting, however, as Table 5.4 points out. Although both those with high incomes and those with high levels of education are more inclined to vote for rightist parties,

Table 5.2
Income Explained by EGP Class and Education (regression coefficients with standard errors in parentheses, 1956-1990, N=93,567 respondents and 15 countries)

Independent variables	Null model		Model 1		Model 2	
Constant	3.146***	(0.297)	3.146***	(0.297)	3.146***	(0.297)
Higher professionals (I)[1]			0		0	
Lower professionals (II)			-0.222***	(0.011)	-0.206***	(0.011)
Nonmanual workers (III)			-0.568***	(0.012)	-0.380***	(0.012)
Petty bourgeoisie (IV)			-0.427***	(0.009)	-0.242***	(0.010)
Higher working class (V)			-0.179***	(0.008)	-0.089***	(0.008)
Skilled manual workers (VI)			-0.612***	(0.011)	-0.368***	(0.011)
Semi and unskilled manual workers (VII)			-0.867***	(0.011)	-0.545***	(0.012)
Education					0.587***	(0.008)
Variance country level	0.772	(0.457)	0.771	(0.456)	0.771	(0.456)
Variance year level	1.429***	(0.248)	1.430***	(0.248)	1.430***	(0.248)
Variance individual level	5.405***	(0.025)	4.948***	(0.023)	4.695***	(0.022)
Deviance	423,871.7		415,616.9		410,698.2	

* p< 0.05; ** p< 0.01; *** p< 0.001
1. Reference category

Table 5.3
Rightist Voting Explained by EGP Class
(regression coefficients and residual variances with standard errors in parentheses, 1956-1990, N=93,567 respondents and 15 countries)

Independent variables	Model 1		Model 2	
Constant	4.796***	(0.191)	4.796***	(0.191)
Fixed effects				
Higher professionals (I)[1]	0		0	
Lower professionals (II)	-0.086***	(0.018)	-0.090***	(0.018)
Nonmanual workers (III)	-0.139***	(0.022)	-0.141***	(0.022)
Petty bourgeoisie (IV)	0.058	(0.029)	0.055	(0.029)
Higher working class (V)	-0.083***	(0.023)	-0.084***	(0.023)
Skilled manual workers (VI)	-0.313***	(0.052)	-0.313***	(0.052)
Semi and unskilled manual workers (VII)	-0.307***	(0.057)	-0.308***	(0.057)
Year	0.020	(0.024)	0.020	(0.024)
Interactions				
Year x higher professionals (I)[1]			0	
Year x lower professionals (II)			-0.011	(0.008)
Year x nonmanual workers (III)			0.019*	(0.009)
Year x petty bourgeoisie (IV)			0.013	(0.008)
Year x higher working class (V)			0.011	(0.008)
Year x skilled manual workers (VI)			0.037**	(0.009)
Year x semi and unskilled manual workers (VII)			0.033**	(0.010)
Variance random slopes country level				
Higher professionals (I)[1]	0		0	
Lower professionals (II)	0.003	(0.002)	0.003	(0.002)
Nonmanual workers (III)	0.005*	(0.002)	0.005*	(0.002)

Table 5.3 (cont.)

Petty bourgeoisie (IV)	0.009*	(0.004)	0.009*	(0.004)
Higher working class (V)	0.005	(0.003)	0.005	(0.003)
Skilled manual workers (VI)	0.038*	(0.015)	0.037*	(0.015)
Semi and unskilled manual workers (VII)	0.045*	(0.018)	0.044*	(0.017)
Variance random slopes year level				
Higher professionals (I)[1]	0		0	
Lower professionals (II)	0.001	(0.001)	0.000	(0.000)
Nonmanual workers (III)	0.001*	(0.000)	0.001*	(0.000)
Petty bourgeoisie (IV)	0.001	(0.001)	0.001	(0.001)
Higher working class (V)	0.002*	(0.001)	0.002*	(0.001)
Skilled manual workers (VI)	0.002*	(0.001)	0.001	(0.001)
Semi and unskilled manual workers (VII)	0.002*	(0.001)	0.001	(0.001)
Variance country level	0.523**	(0.191)	0.523**	(0.191)
Variance year level	0.040***	(0.007)	0.040***	(0.007)
Variance individual level	2.036***	(0.009)	2.036***	(0.009)
Deviance	332,794.4		332,746.8	

* $p < 0.05$; ** $p < 0.01$; *** $p < 0.001$

1. Reference category

Using rightist voting as the dependent variable and six EGP class dummies as the independent ones, we next turn to the relationship between EGP class and voting behavior and the way this relationship has changed in the postwar era. It is evident that the skilled, semi- and unskilled manual workers vote for leftist parties more often than the middle class (Table 5.3, Model 1) and it is also clear that those traditional alignments have weakened across time (Model 2). There is nothing surprising about this finding, of course, because Nieuwbeerta (1995, 1996, 2001, Nieuwbeerta and De Graaf 1999) has previously published it, based on an analysis of the same data.

Table 5.4
Rightist Voting Explained by Income and Education (regression coefficients and residual variables with standard errors in parentheses, 1956-1990, N=93,567 respondents and 15 countries)

Independent variables	Model 1		Model 2		Model 3	
Constant	4.796***	(0.191)	4.796***	(0.191)	4.796***	(0.191)
Fixed effects						
Income	0.099**	(0.027)	0.098**	(0.027)	0.101**	(0.028)
Education	0.104*	(0.048)	0.100*	(0.048)	0.099*	(0.046)
Year	0.020	(0.024)	0.020	(0.024)	0.020	(0.024)
Interactions						
Education x year			-0.037**	(0.009)	-0.040**	(0.009)
Income x year					0.024*	(0.010)
Variance random slopes country level						
Income	0.007	(0.004)	0.007	(0.004)	0.007	(0.004)

Table 5.4 (cont.)

Education	0.031*	(0.013)	0.028*	(0.011)	0.028*	(0.011)
Variance random slopes year level						
Income	0.006***	(0.001)	0.006***	(0.001)	0.005***	(0.001)
Education	0.004**	(0.001)	0.003**	(0.001)	0.003**	(0.001)
Variance country level	0.523**	(0.191)	0.523**	(0.191)	0.523**	(0.191)
Variance year level	0.040***	(0.007)	0.040***	(0.007)	0.040***	(0.007)
Variance individual level	2.114***	(0.009)	2.114***	(0.009)	2.114***	(0.009)
Deviance	336,131.1		336,114.1		336,108.5	

* p< 0.05; ** p< 0.01; *** p< 0.001

Figure 5.2
Trends in the Relationships of Income and Education with Rightist Voting

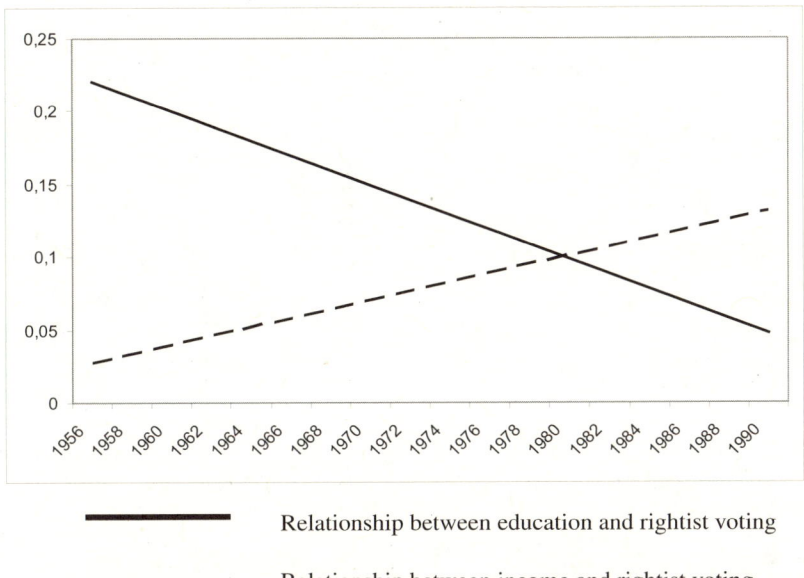

———— Relationship between education and rightist voting

— — — Relationship between income and rightist voting

both of those relationships have changed across time, albeit in different directions. The significant cross-level interactions of education and income with year (Models 2 and 3) point out that those with low levels of education have come to vote more *rightist*, while those with low incomes have come to vote more *leftist* across the years.

Figure 5.2 illustrates these trends. The dotted line indicates the increasing strength of the relation between income and rightist voting, while the solid line shows the decreasing strength of the relationship between education and rightist voting. Put differently, since World War II, the poor (rich) increasingly voted left (right) wing, while the lower (higher) educated increasingly voted right (left) wing. This is obviously not what one would expect if both of these two variables unambiguously indicated class. Indeed, as explained above, whereas the former development can be interpreted as an increase in class voting, the latter rather needs to be interpreted as an increase in cultural voting. This brings us to our principal question: has the decline of the relationship between EGP class and voting behavior indeed been caused by this increase of cultural voting?

Obviously, the increasing tendency of the working class to vote for

Table 5.5
Rightist Voting Explained by EGP Class, Income and Education
(regression coefficients and residual variances with standard errors in parentheses, 1956-1990, N=93,567 respondents and 15 countries).

Independent variables	Model 1		Model 2		Model 3	
Constant	4.796***	(0.191)	4.796***	(0.191)	4.796***	(0.191)
Fixed effects						
Higher professionals (I)[1]	0		0		0	
Lower professionals (II)	-0.077***	(0.018)	-0.072***	(0.018)	-0.072***	(0.018)
Nonmanual workers (III)	-0.118***	(0.024)	-0.101***	(0.022)	-0.101***	(0.022)
Petty bourgeoisie (IV)	0.079**	(0.030)	0.108**	(0.029)	0.108**	(0.029)
Higher working class (V)	-0.076**	(0.023)	-0.071**	(0.023)	-0.071**	(0.023)
Skilled manual workers (VI)	-0.284***	(0.053)	-0.256***	(0.052)	-0.256***	(0.052)
Semi and unskilled manual workers (VII)	-0.272***	(0.058)	-0.244***	(0.057)	-0.244***	(0.057)
Income	0.097**	(0.005)	0.086**	(0.019)	0.086**	(0.019)
Education	-0.005	(0.006)	0.020	(0.038)	0.020	(0.038)
Year	0.020	(0.024)	0.020	(0.024)	0.020	(0.024)

Table 5.5 (cont.)

Interactions						
Year x higher professionals (I)[1]	0		0		0	
Year x lower professionals (II)	-0.010	(0.008)	-0.011	(0.008)	-0.012	(0.008)
Year x nonmanual workers (III)	0.019*	(0.008)	0.016	(0.009)	0.012	(0.009)
Year x petty bourgeoisie (IV)	0.007	(0.008)	0.003	(0.009)	-0.002	(0.009)
Year x higher working class (V)	0.011	(0.008)	0.008	(0.007)	0.006	(0.007)
Year x skilled manual workers (VI)	0.034**	(0.009)	0.030**	(0.009)	0.024**	(0.009)
Year x semi and unskilled manual workers (VII)	0.019**	(0.010)	0.025**	(0.010)	0.017	(0.010)
Year x income			0.025**	(0.009)	0.029**	(0.009)
Year x education					-0.038**	(0.009)
Variance random slopes country level						
Higher professionals (I)[1]	0		0		0	
Lower professionals (II)	0.003	(0.002)	0.002*	(0.001)	0.002*	(0.001)
Nonmanual workers (III)	0.005	(0.003)	0.001	(0.001)	0.001	(0.001)

Table 5.5 (cont.)

Petty bourgeoisie (IV)	0.010*	(0.005)	0.014*	(0.006)	0.014*	(0.006)
Higher working class (V)	0.005	(0.003)	0.004*	(0.002)	0.004*	(0.002)
Skilled manual workers (VI)	0.038**	(0.015)	0.019*	(0.008)	0.019*	(0.008)
Semi and unskilled manual workers (VII)	0.046*	(0.018)	0.023*	(0.009)	0.023*	(0.009)
Income	0.003	(0.002)	0.003	(0.002)	0.003	(0.002)
Education	0.021*	(0.009)	0.018*	(0.008)	0.018*	(0.008)
Variance random slopes year level						
Higher professionals (I)[1]	0		0		0	
Lower professionals (II)	0.000	(0.000)	0.000	(0.000)	0.000	(0.000)
Nonmanual workers (III)	0.000	(0.000)	0.000	(0.000)	0.000	(0.000)
Petty bourgeoisie (IV)	0.001	(0.001)	0.001	(0.001)	0.001	(0.001)
Higher working class (V)	0.002	(0.001)	0.001	(0.001)	0.001	(0.001)
Skilled manual workers (VI)	0.001*	(0.000)	0.001*	(0.000)	0.001*	(0.000)
Semi and unskilled manual workers (VII)	0.001	(0.001)	0.001	(0.000)	0.001	(0.001)
Income	0.003**	(0.001)	0.003**	(0.001)	0.003**	(0.001)

Table 5.5 (cont.)

Education	0.004**	(0.001)	0.004**	(0.001)	0.003**	(0.001)
Variance country level	0.523**	(0.191)	0.523**	(0.191)	0.523**	(0.191)
Variance year level	0.040***	(0.007)	0.040***	(0.007)	0.040***	(0.007)
Variance individual level	2.028***	(0.009)	2.014***	(0.009)	2.014***	(0.009)
Deviance	332,375.6		331,881.0		331,881.0	

* p< 0.05; ** p< 0.01; *** p< 0.001

1. Reference category

rightist parties cannot be explained from the increasing tendency of those with low incomes to vote for parties on the left (Table 5.5, Model 2). As expected, however, the increase of cultural voting, i.e., the increased tendency of those with low levels of education to vote for rightist parties, accounts for most of the shift of the working class towards rightist parties (Model 3). Although the traditional class alignments have clearly weakened in the postwar era, in short, this has not been caused by a decline of class voting, but by an increase of cross-cutting cultural voting.

Conclusion

What Stonecash has demonstrated for the United States applies more generally: class voting has not declined during the postwar era, but has even become stronger. The suggestion to the contrary has been informed by studies of the development of the bivariate relationship between occupation-based class categories (especially the EGP class schema) and voting behavior. This type of class measure inevitably and wrongly mixes up class voting, driven by class-based economic interests, and cross-cutting cultural voting, driven by a cultural dynamics that is instead rooted in educational differences. It as such precludes valid conclusions as to whether the decline of the familiar alignments denotes a decline of class voting or an increase of cultural voting.

Our findings, relying on income to indicate class more validly, and acknowledging the double role of education in driving class voting as well as cross-cutting cultural voting, leave little to the imagination. The gradual erosion of the pattern of a leftist-voting working class and a rightist-voting middle class has been caused by an increase of cross-cutting cultural voting, driven by a cultural dynamics that is rooted in educational differences. Class voting has not declined, but has in fact become even stronger in the postwar era.

The intellectual consensus that has emerged since Clark and Lipset sparked the "Death of Class Debate" in the beginning of the 1990s does not hold that class is actually dead, to be sure, but rather that it is dying a slow—and perhaps painful—death. Our findings necessitate a critical reassessment of this consensus. They point out not so much that class is "dying," after all, but rather that increasing cultural voting has systematically been misinterpreted as a decline of class voting due to an invalid measurement practice that has become an intellectual routine since Alford's pioneering work.

Note

1. Our departure from Nieuwbeerta's operationalization, and especially our decision to code the political parties according to the left-right self-placements of their constituencies, causes a substantial increase of the number of missing values: 33 of the 113 original datasets are excluded, causing Sweden (with three datasets) to disappear from our analysis altogether.

6

The Working Class and the Welfare State: Judgments on the Rights and Obligations of the Unemployed

Introduction

The working class is generally held to have a special interest in the maintenance and expansion of the welfare state, because the latter entails a decommodification of labor (Esping-Andersen 1990) and hence a weakening of the link between work and income. Yet, studies typically fail to find strong support among the working class for the welfare state and for the severing of this link, as Van Oorschot (1998: 72) rightly points out.

This finding seems inconsistent with the class theory of politics, which conceives of maintenance and expansion of the welfare state as a key interest of those with a weak position in economic life. What makes this finding even more puzzling, of course, is that the working class is nevertheless—and consistent with the class theory of politics—more economically egalitarian than any other class, as we have seen in Chapters 2 and 3 (see also Marshall et al. 1988: 179-183, Middendorp 1991, Scheepers et al. 1992, Weakliem and Heath 1994, Elchardus 1996, De Witte and Billiet 1999, Edlund 1999, Svallfors 1999). How to explain this intriguing paradox that the working class is more economically egalitarian than society's other classes, yet not more strongly in favor of severing the link between work and income?

To solve this paradox it first of all needs to be emphasized that the welfare state never simply boils down to severing the link between work and income. Indeed,

> One of the most important questions which all societies with systems of social policy have faced is how to provide support for the needy without, at the same time, undermining their incentive to work. (…) Although most industrial societies have accepted

at least some degree of responsibility for the "impotent poor"—the sick and disabled, the elderly and children—the question of how to deal with the "able-bodied" poor has always been a matter of controversy (Higgins 1981: 100).

Although a less lenient treatment of the "able-bodied" or "valid" poor as compared to the "impotent" or "invalid" poor particularly characterized the poor laws from the sixteenth century onwards (e.g., Slack 1988, Lis and Soly 1979), this distinction has not disappeared in contemporary welfare states. More than that: notions of deservingness have become markedly more politically salient in Europe since the 1980s (Houtman 1994), with especially rightist-populist parties casting those on welfare as a new parasitic class and with the working class in particular susceptible to this discourse.

Hypotheses

Asking attention for the double meaning of the word "social," Jones suggests that the welfare state is not simply a regime of care, but one of disciplinarization, too. She raises the question whether "'social policy' (is) to be perceived as being *primarily* geared to promoting the interests of society as a whole, or as being *primarily* geared to protecting the welfare of individual members within it" (1985: 14). Indeed, besides granting all sorts of social rights to citizens, the welfare state (conceived in the widest sense so as to also include state-supported systems of education, health care, etc.) also aims to provide (post-)industrial societies with skilled, healthy and motivated workforces (Wilensky 1975, Higgins 1981: 117-121).

The precarious balance of rights and obligations that results from this dual aim is most visible in case of the unemployed and is expressed in the legal notion of "suitable employment" (Dutch: *passende arbeid*), which captures the balance between the right of the unemployed to a social security benefit and their obligation to work. It expresses that although the unemployed have a right to an unemployment benefit, this right is conditional on their willingness to accept a job (Houtman 1994: 11-28). Although with the emergence of the modern welfare state the idea of "care as right" has replaced that of "care as favor" (Marshall 1965, Zijderveld 1999), criteria of deservingness thus still play a major role in systems of social security for the unemployed (Macarov 1980). Unconditionally granting rights to unemployment benefits is the exception rather than the rule and the more these rights are made dependent on criteria of deservingness, the more the welfare state's disciplinary face overshadows its caring one.

Our finding that occupation-based measurements of social class mix up the strength of one's position on the labor market ("class"), affecting economic egalitarianism/conservatism, and cultural capital, strongly related to authoritarianism/libertarianism, suggests a plausible explanation for the remarkable lack of working-class support for the welfare state. Just like a zero-relationship between EGP class and voting behavior does not necessarily contradict the assumption that a weak position on the labor market leads to leftist voting, a zero-relationship between class and preferences regarding the strength of the link between work and income does after all not necessarily contradict working-class economic egalitarianism. Whereas class voting is easily made invisible by equally strong cross-cutting cultural voting, a working-class preference for a weaker link between work and income, based in its class interests and economic egalitarianism, is easily made invisible by a simultaneous preference for strict criteria of deservingness that is based in its limited cultural capital and related authoritarianism.

This line of reasoning is of course consistent with the well-known circumstance that authoritarianism is strongly and positively related to the rejection of all sorts of out-groups and unconventional life-styles that happen to have become salient for whatever reason—e.g., homosexuals, emancipated women, ethnic minorities and immigrants, AIDS patients, etcetera (e.g., Middendorp 1991, Eisinga and Scheepers 1989, Dekker and Ester 1993). Now that public discourse has since the 1980s increasingly framed the crisis of the welfare state in moral terms of deservingness, it is likely that working-class authoritarianism detracts from any preference it may otherwise have for severing the link between work and income.

We study in this chapter whether this is indeed the case, i.e., whether its weak economic position leads the working class to emphasize the rights of the unemployed, while its limited cultural capital and related authoritarianism leads it to emphasize their obligations. If confirmed, these two cross-cutting tendencies easily result in a working class that does not differ from society's other classes when it comes to the preferred strength of the link between work and income, thus providing a solution to the puzzle addressed in this chapter.

Data and Measurement

To test this theory, we analyze the data we have already used in Chapter 2 and that have been collected in the Netherlands in 1997. *Authoritarianism* is measured by means of the short version of the F-scale (Adorno et al., 1950) that is also used there (Cronbach's $\alpha=0.79$) and *economic egalitarianism* with the same six Likert items (Cronbach's α=0.71).[1] Table 6.1 below contains these two sets of items and the results of a factor analysis. Both scales have been constructed by linearly combining the two sets of relevant items and recoding them for our purposes here so as to range from 0 to 10. High scores indicate libertarianism and economic egalitarianism, respectively, and the relationship between the two scales is exactly -0.00, confirming their independence.

The measurements of *social class* (EGP class schema), *education, income, wage dependence, cultural participation,* and *job insecurity* are basically identical to those used in Chapter 2. We have however transformed cultural participation and job insecurity so as to make them range from 0 to 10 to allow somewhat more meaningful comparisons between the seven EGP classes.

Judgments on the rights and obligations of the unemployed have been measured by means of three types of questions, all of which have been validated previously (Houtman 1994, 1997). First, acceptance or rejection of a *right to an unemployment benefit* and an *obligation to work* have been ascertained by agreement or disagreement with two statements: "People receiving an unemployment benefit ought to be burning with shame for that" and "People receiving an unemployment benefit should have the right to choose freely whether they want to live on this benefit or on paid work." Because the key characteristic of a right is that there is no need to feel ashamed when one makes use of it, agreement with the former statement indicates a rejection of the right to an unemployment benefit. Obviously, disagreement with the latter statement indicates an acceptance of the obligation to work. Answers to those two questions have been combined into three categories: 1) acceptance of both principles (83 percent), 2) acceptance of the obligation to work and rejection of the right to an unemployment benefit (6 percent), and 3) rejection of the obligation to work and acceptance of the right to an unemployment benefit (11 percent). The fourth possible combination—i.e., the rejection of both the obligation to work and the right to an unemployment benefit—is treated as missing, because it applies to only three respondents.

Second, respondents have been asked to evaluate two proposals to introduce an alternative system of social security, in which either the right to an unemployment benefit or the obligation to work is emphasized at the expense of the other: a *guaranteed basic income* (e.g., Van Parijs 1992) and a system of *workfare* (e.g., Mead 1986). Both systems were introduced to respondents by first stating that "some people in The Netherlands are proposing to change the prevailing system of social

Table 6.1
Factor Analysis of Items Indicating Economic Egalitarianism and Libertarianism (Varimax rotation)

Items	Factor 1	Factor 2
The state should make social benefits higher.	-0.22	0.56
There is no longer any real poverty in the Netherlands.	0.11	-0.52
Large income differences are unfair because in essence everyone is equal.	0.05	0.77
Nowadays, workers no longer have to fight for an equal position in society.	0.07	-0.52
The state should intervene to reduce income differences.	0.12	0.82
Companies should be obliged to allow their employees to share in profits.	0.17	0.52
More and more people have recently begun to interfere with matters that ought to be personal and private.	0.43	0.22
Most people are disappointing when you get to know them better.	0.59	0.20
Young people sometimes have rebellious ideas but as they grow older they ought to grow out of them and adjust to reality.	0.61	-0.17
Our social problems would be largely solved, if we could only somehow remove criminal and anti-social elements from society.	0.68	-0.12
What we need are fewer laws and agencies and more courageous, tireless leaders who people can have faith in.	0.69	0.00
People with bad manners, habits and upbringing can hardly be expected to know how to associate with decent people.	0.53	-0.02
There are two kinds of people, strong ones and weak ones.	0.61	0.03
Sexual offences such as raping and sexually assaulting children warrant more severe punishment than just prison sentences; criminals like these should be given corporal punishment in public.	0.63	-0.01
If people would talk less and work harder, everything would be better.	0.61	-0.17
Eigenvalue	3.38	2.54
R^2	0.23	0.17
Cronbach's α	0.79	0.71

security" and then briefly describing the changes proposed by "these people."[2] Answers to those two questions have been combined into four categories: 1) a positive evaluation of workfare and a negative evaluation of a basic income (42 percent), 2) a positive evaluation of workfare and an undecided evaluation of a basic income ("don't know") (9 percent), 3) an either positive or negative evaluation of both alternative systems of social security (40 percent), and 4) a positive evaluation of a basic income and a negative or undecided evaluation of workfare (10 percent).

Third, we have used evaluations of the *fairness of cutting an unemployment benefit if a job offer is declined*. Respondents have been asked to evaluate four specific cases in which an unemployed person refuses to accept a job offer (see Figure 6.1 for an example).[3] More specifically, they have been asked whether imposing a sanction by cutting the unemployment benefit for a period of three months was just and, if so, how high this sanction should be. Nine response categories have been used, ranging from 1 ("cut deemed unfair") through 9 ("cut of more than Dfl. 750 monthly deemed fair").

Finally, the evaluations of the four cases of work refusal and the two other variables described above have been analyzed by means of HOMALS (SPSS), which yields a well interpretable first dimension with an eigenvalue of 0.54. Discrimination measures are 0.29 for the combined evaluation of the two alternative systems of social security, 0.21 for the combined evaluation of the obligation to work and the right to an unemployment benefit and higher than 0.50 for the judgments on the four cases of work refusal.[4] Highest scores are assigned to those who

Figure 6.1
Example of One of the Four Cases Used

Occupation/education:	psychologist (university training)
Unemployment duration:	2 years (has never been employed)
Age:	25 years
Household composition:	single – no children (unemployment benefit Dfl. 1,315 monthly)
Job offered:	parking lot attendant
Net monthly income:	Dfl. 1,700 monthly

reject the right of the unemployed to a social security benefit and accept their obligation to work, those who reject a guaranteed basic income and accept a system of workfare, and those who feel that large cuts in cases of job refusal are justified. The measure's reliability is 0.81 (Cronbach's α). In this case, too, scores have been transformed into a scale ranging from 0 to 10. Highest scores indicate the strongest tendency to make unemployment benefits conditional on strict criteria of deservingness and hence the weakest tendency to sever the link between work and income.

Results

EGP Class, Economic Egalitarianism, Authoritarianism, and Judgments on the Rights and Obligations of the Unemployed

We first inspect the relationships between EGP class on the one hand and economic egalitarianism/conservatism, authoritarianism/libertarianism, and judgments on the rights and obligations of the unemployed on the other. Table 6.2 points out that the working class—especially Class VI and Class VII—is neither more, nor less inclined than the other classes to sever the link between work and income. There are hardly any differences between the seven EGP classes when it comes to the degree to which they emphasize the rights or the obligations of the unemployed and variance explained is close to zero. It is obvious that those findings confirm Van Oorschot's (1998: 72) claim that the working class is not the passionate supporter of relatively unconditionally granting social rights to citizens that it is so often assumed to be.

Table 6.2 also points out that this inconspicuous position when it comes to judgments on the rights and obligations of the unemployed contrasts with working-class economic egalitarianism. Four EGP classes score above the grand mean of 4.89. This applies only weakly to Class III and especially Class V, but the two EGP classes that together constitute the uncontested working class, Class VI and Class VII, are clearly more economically egalitarian than the other EGP classes. They deviate especially from the self-employed (Class IV), who are least likely to support the idea that the state has a responsibility in reducing the income differences that result from free-market competition. Although these findings confirm that the working class supports economic redistribution more than the other classes, it should also be noted that differences between the seven EGP classes are quite small with a variance explained of merely 7 percent.

With 12 percent of the variance explained, differences with regard to authoritarianism/libertarianism are more substantial. Class I and Class

Table 6.2
Emphasis on Obligations of the Unemployed, Economic Egalitarianism, and Libertarianism Explained by EGP Class (deviations from means)

EGP Class	Emphasis obligations unemployed	Economic egalitarianism	Libertarianism
Higher professionals (I)	-0.37	-0.27	0.97
Lower professionals (II)	0.05	-0.30	0.42
Nonmanual workers (III)	-0.09	0.24	-0.22
Petty bourgeoisie (IV)	0.61	-1.26	-0.25
Higher working class (V)	0.37	0.04	-0.16
Skilled workers (VI)	-0.35	0.67	-0.99
Semi and unskilled workers (VII)	0.15	0.75	-1.03
Mean	5.49	4.89	5.53
η	0.12 (n.s.)	0.25***	0.35***
R^2	0.01	0.07***	0.12***
N	706	697	682

n.s.: $p>0.05$; *** $p<0.001$

II are more libertarian than average and highest levels of authoritarianism are found within the working class (Class VI and Class VII). We find exactly the pattern pointed out by Lipset in the 1950s, in short: the working class is not only characterized by a high level of economic egalitarianism, but by a high level of authoritarianism, too.

EGP Class, Labor Market Position, and Cultural Capital

As we have seen in Chapter 2, working-class authoritarianism, unlike working-class egalitarianism, does not stem from its weak position on the labor market, but from its limited cultural capital. Indeed, those who are coded as belonging to the working class in the EGP class schema are not only characterized by a weak labor-market position, but by limited cultural capital, too (Table 6.3).

Table 6.3
Net Personal Income, Job Insecurity, Education, and Cultural Participation Explained by EGP Class (deviations from means)

EGP Class	Income	Income (corrected)[1]	Job insecurity	Education	Cultural particip.
Higher professionals (I)	991	914	-0.11	1.3	0.98
Lower professionals (II)	224	261	-0.36	0.8	0.49
Nonmanual workers (III)	-621	-340	0.47	-0.5	-0.15
Petty bourgeoisie (IV)	556	-168	-0.53	-0.3	0.49
Higher working class (V)	228	38	-0.11	-0.4	-0.76
Skilled workers (VI)	-512	-665	-0.12	-1.1	-1.48
Semi and unskilled workers (VII)	-692	-718	0.47	-1.7	-1.05
Mean	3,080	3,080	1.65	4.5	2.97
η	0.53***	0.47***	0.23***	0.59***	0.37***
R^2	0.28***	0.48***	0.05***	0.34***	0.14***
N	678	678	706	689	705

*** $p < 0.001$

[1] Corrected (by means of covariates) for age, sex, and number of weekly working hours

Table 6.3 does not present differences between the seven EGP classes regarding wage dependence, because the latter is used in coding the EGP class schema. All members of Class IV, for instance, are self-employed, whereas workers (Class VI and Class VII) work for wages by definition.

Almost 30 percent of personal income differences can be explained from EGP class. This is of course not surprising, because the ability to explain income differences is typically regarded a *conditio sine qua non* for the validity of class measures (e.g., Marshall et al. 1988, Wright 1979, 1985, Middendorp and Meloen 1990) as well as an argument for the contemporary existence of social classes—in the Marxian sense of *Klassen an sich* rather than *Klassen für sich* (e.g., Wright 1979, Hout et al. 1993). Controlling for age, gender, and number of working hours—three variables known to affect income[5]—hardly affects the income differences between the seven EGP classes.[6] On average, then, members of Class VI and Class VII, the working class, have lower incomes than members of the others EGP classes.

There are hardly differences regarding job insecurity between the seven EGP classes. Only 5 percent of those differences can be explained from EGP class, with especially Class III and Class VII characterized by job insecurity. This is an important finding, because one may doubt the validity of a class measure that fails to capture this vital dimension of economic inequality.[7] As we see it, the circumstance that job insecurity is only weakly related to occupation calls for a reconsideration of the sociological convention of coding occupations into classes rather than assessing the strengths of labor market positions in a more direct fashion. The findings of the preceding chapters obviously make such a reconsideration even more urgent: because occupation-based class schemas inevitably mix up the strength of one's labor market position with cultural capital, increases in cultural voting have typically been misinterpreted as declines of class voting. Whereas no less than 34 percent of the educational differences and 14 percent of those pertaining to cultural participation are also captured by the distinction between the seven EGP classes, the latter after all also differ substantially in those two respects. The largely occupation-based EGP class schema mixes up class in an economic sense with cultural capital, in short.

Judgments on the Rights and Obligations of the Unemployed Explained

The foregoing suggests indeed that the inconspicuous position of the working class when it comes to judgments on the rights and obligations of the unemployed stems from two contradictory tendencies. Does working-class economic egalitarianism, stemming from its weak labor-market position, lead it to emphasize the rights of the unemployed, whereas its authoritarianism, connected to its limited cultural capital, leads it to emphasize their obligations? To answer this question, we use OLS-regression to construct a path model that depicts how the explicit indicators for class and cultural capital affect economic egalitarianism and authoritarianism and how the latter affect judgments on the rights and obligations of the unemployed (Figure 6.2).

A low family income, a low level of education, job insecurity, and wage dependence—in short: a weak class position—all lead to stronger economic egalitarianism. Although none of these effects is very strong,

Figure 6.2
Emphasis on the Obligations of the Unemployed Explained
(only significant paths (p<0.05) shown, R^2 emphasis on obligations of the unemployed: 0.14, R^2 economic egalitarianism: 0.09, R^2 libertarianism: 0.22, N=644)

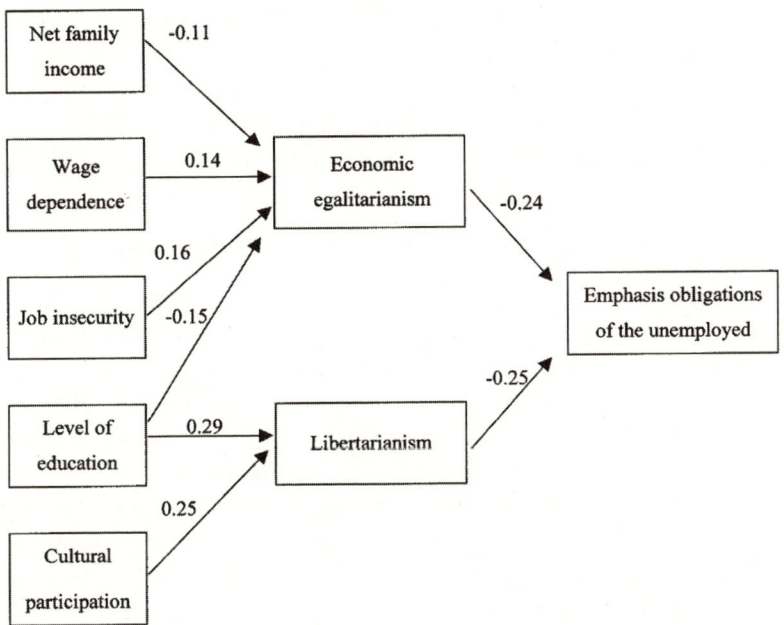

variance explained is slightly higher than in the preceding analysis with EGP class as the independent variable. Cultural participation, the only variable that does not indicate social class, has no effect whatsoever on economic egalitarianism. As we have discussed in more detail in Chapter 2, those findings are consistent with the class theory of politics: the working class supports economic redistribution because of its class-based economic interests.[8]

We have also already pointed out in Chapter 2 that the negative effect of education on authoritarianism cannot be interpreted as a class effect, because neither income, nor job insecurity, nor wage dependence—all three unambiguous class indicators—affects authoritarianism, whereas a high level of cultural participation detracts from the latter almost as much as a high level of education. Unlike working-class economic egalitarianism, then, working-class authoritarianism stems from its limited amount of cultural capital rather than its weak labor-market position.[9]

Finally, none of the indicators for class and cultural capital affects judgments on the rights and obligations of the unemployed directly. A low family income, a low level of education, job insecurity, and wage dependence all increase economic egalitarianism, which in its turn strengthens the emphasis on the rights of the unemployed. Reversely, a limited amount of cultural capital—a low level of education and limited cultural participation—increases authoritarianism, which in turn strengthens the emphasis on the obligations of the unemployed. As a result of these two cross-cutting tendencies, the working class does not emerge as the ardent supporter of severing the link between work and income it is so often assumed to be.

Conclusion: Distributive and Retributive Justice

In this chapter, we have explained the paradox that although the working class is more economically egalitarian, it nevertheless does not favor weakening the link between work and income more than society's other classes and hence does not more strongly emphasize the rights of the unemployed at the cost of their obligations either. Just like rightist voting by the working class, its emphasis on the obligations of the unemployed is caused by its limited amount of cultural capital and the authoritarianism tied to it. This means that its emphasis on the obligations of the unemployed does not contradict the key assumption of the class theory of politics that a weak position on the labor market leads to a preference for economic egalitarianism. More than that: its class-based economic interests do in fact lead the working class to prefer a weakening of the link between work and income by emphasizing the rights of the unemployed. The point is, again, that these two cross-cutting tendencies cancel each other out, resulting in a working-class position on judgments on the rights and obligations of the unemployed that is basically identical to that of the middle class.

What our analysis reveals, in short, is that judgments on the rights and obligations of the unemployed are not simply judgments of *distributive justice*, i.e., judgments about the just distribution of scarce and highly valued goods. They are simultaneously judgments of *retributive justice*, i.e., judgments about the justice of sanctioning those who deviate from group norms (e.g., Benn and Peters 1977: 173, Buchanan and Mathieu 1986: 13-14, Cook and Hegtvedt 1983: 220). Once we give this ambiguity of judgments on the rights and obligations of the unemployed its due, the paradox that the working class is more economically egalitarian than society's other classes, yet not more strongly favors severing the link between work and income, disappears.

Notes

1. The short version of the F-scale has been combined with three others measures in Chapter 2 to arrive at the measurement of authoritarian/libertarianism used there. Although it is used alone here—and as suggested by the four high factor loadings mentioned in Chapter 2—this difference does not substantially affect the results of the statistical analyses.
2. In both questions, it was made clear that the level of the benefits themselves would remain unchanged.
3. In all four cases, work that requires only a minimum of training was chosen, to ensure that anyone could plausibly perform it. The mentioned levels of the unemployment benefits are derived from the levels that applied at the time of data collection (Public Assistance Act). Respondents were asked to assume that in none of the cases special justifications for declining the job, such as health problems or necessary long distance travel to and from work, applied.
4. In case of the four cases of work refusal, the higher the cut deemed fair, the higher the quantification of the corresponding category. The quantifications of the categories of the two other variables are consistent with this. Combined evaluations of the right to an unemployment benefit and the obligation to work: 1) acceptance of both principles (0.10), 2) acceptance of the obligation to work and rejection of the right to an unemployment benefit (0.72), and 3) rejection of the obligation to work and acceptance of the right to an unemployment benefit (-1.27). Combined evaluations of the two alternative systems of social security: 1) workfare evaluated positively and basic income evaluated negatively (0.52), 2) workfare evaluated positively and basic income undecided ("don't know") (0.19), 3) both workfare and basic income evaluated either positively or negatively (-0.35), and 4) basic income evaluated positively and workfare evaluated either negatively or undecided (-1.12).
5. Given the type of work one does, one's income tends to be higher when one is older, male and, obviously, working more hours per week. As to the income differences between men and women, the reader is referred to Schippers (1995).
6. As expected, young people, women, and those working a limited number of hours per week, earn lower incomes than the others do. The combined effect of those three variables is considerable, as the rise of the variance explained from 28 percent to 48 percent indicates (the three separate effects are not displayed in Table 6.3). Nevertheless, the initial income differences between the seven classes are hardly caused by disproportional numbers of young people, women, and part-time workers within the classes with the lowest average incomes. There is one exception to this, however, as the remarkably low mean income of class III (routine nonmanual) is caused by this phenomenon. That the income of the self-employed (Class IV) declines dramatically after controlling for those variables is, of course, caused by their relatively high number of weekly working hours.
7. Steijn and Houtman (1998) have found the same.
8. One of us has demonstrated elsewhere that income, education, job insecurity, and wage dependence account for all of the differences between the seven EGP classes regarding economic egalitarianism (Houtman 2001, 2003: 24-46, 2004).
9. Hardly surprising, then, education and cultural participation explain substantially more variance in authoritarianism/libertarianism than EGP class (22 percent as compared to 12 percent). Education and cultural participation account for all of the differences between the seven EGP classes regarding authoritarianism/libertarianism, too (Houtman 2001, 2003: 24-46, 2004).

7

Is Working-Class Economic Egalitarianism Really that Politically Progressive? Economic Populism, Egalitarianism, and Political Progressiveness

Introduction

Although the working class supports economic redistribution, this does not simply mean that it also supports the welfare state, as we have seen, because its limited cultural capital and related authoritarianism makes it reluctant to sever the link between work and income. Indeed, the more the welfare state is construed in moral terms, the more working-class authoritarianism undermines support for the welfare state, thus effectively driving a wedge between the latter and economic egalitarianism.

Already in the 1970s, Middendorp (1978) has demonstrated that working-class aversion to social inequality is not necessarily translated into adherence to a full-fledged leftist ideology. And in the United States, Horowitz has critiqued Lipset's position that the working class—albeit authoritarian when it comes to cultural issues—stands out as firmly progressive when it comes to issues of economic distribution, pointing out that "it is far from self-evident that the new working class is as inextricably committed to a Leninist notion of 'economism' as Lipset believes" (1977: 101). More than that: rightist-populist political discourse in Europe easily produces a working class that supports economic redistribution, while simultaneously disavowing the welfare state.

Against this background, we study the relationships between economic egalitarianism, support for the welfare state, and political progressiveness in this chapter, focusing on political cultures in which right-authoritarian issues have become highly salient in recent years. We start with an analysis of the relationship between economic egalitarianism and support for the welfare state in Flanders—an instructive case, because its political culture has changed drastically in close connection with a number of successive electoral victories by the rightist-populist Vlaams Blok (since 2004: Vlaams Belang) since the 1980s. Focusing on six European countries in which rightist-populist parties have also been electorally successful in recent years, we then proceed to study whether among the working class economic egalitarianism is less politically progressive than among the middle class.

Economic Populism

Due to its chameleon-like appearance, some authors argue that populism is lacking a stable ideological core and hence needs to be conceived of as a "syndrome" or political "style" rather than a political ideology (e.g., Wiles 1969). Canovan (2002: 32) has recently criticized this position, arguing that populism is a "thin-centered" rather than a "fully fledged" ideology like socialism or liberalism. Populist ideology is not merely "negative" or "anti-establishment," she argues, but possesses a positive core, too, central to which is the appreciation of the "common sense" of ordinary people. This antagonism between "the common people" and "the establishment" constitutes populism's central feature, producing an emphasis on the need to take the spontaneous feelings of "the common people" seriously and to defend their interests against those of privileged elites (Ionescu and Gellner 1969, Betz 1994, Di Tella 1995, Mény and Surel 2000).

Although as a "thin" ideology it does not necessarily imply a particular economic doctrine, contemporary European populism is known for its aversion to taxes, even to such an extent that some (mainly Scandinavian) populist parties were initially known as "anti-tax" parties before they focused on the issue of immigration (Andersen 1992). And indeed, today's new-rightist populists tend to conceive of the tax system and the funding of the welfare state from its revenues as a mechanism of exploitation—an essentially illegitimate means of transferring wealth produced by hard-working common people to unproductive welfare scroungers and bureaucratic and political elites (Taggart 2002: 76). Populism thus entails a rejection of the welfare state, because it is seen as catering to a parasitic class that is sponging on the efforts of the common man rather than to those who "really" need it.[1] Disavowing high taxes, distrusting bureaucratic and political elites, and disliking the welfare state, in short, populism presents itself as the only true advocate of egalitarianism and appeals as such to the interests of the "common man" (Papadopoulos 2001).

Populist aversion to the welfare state needs to be carefully distinguished from *laissez-faire* (neo-)liberalism, then. Driven by anomie and a deeply felt desire for equality, populist ideas about economic distribution tend after all to combine economic egalitarianism with aversion to the welfare state. Such an "economic populism" clearly does not fit into the traditional economic left-right dichotomy, because the latter conceives of economic egalitarianism as "left" and of aversion to the welfare state as "right." This raises the question how these two are related in Flanders, where populism has become increasingly politically salient since the 1980s. Do economic egalitarianism and support for the welfare state still represent the good-old left-right distinction or has this changed in Flanders with the rise of rightist populism?

Data and Measurement

We analyze data from the *APS Survey: Socio-Cultural Shifts in Flanders, 1996*, organized by the Flemish government.[2] This survey was administered face-to-face to a random sample of the Dutch-speaking population with the Belgian nationality, aged 16 to 75, and living in the Flemish Region or in Brussels. Between April and June 1996, the researchers collected 1,577 valid questionnaires (a response rate of 66 percent of first contacts).

A series of nine items measuring economic egalitarianism and aversion to the welfare state will be introduced below, when we discuss our findings. The same goes for anomie.

Class could in this case not be measured by means of the EGP class schema, but respondents have been coded into seven occupational categories that crudely resemble it. With the crudely corresponding EGP classes mentioned in brackets, these are: higher professionals (Class I), lower professionals (Class II), nonmanual workers (Class III), petty bourgeoisie (Class IV), skilled manual workers (Class V and Class VI), unskilled manual workers (Class VII), other wage earners (no EGP equivalent). Class will be entered as a series of seven dummy variables in our regression analyses, treating those who are not gainfully employed as the excluded reference category.

Income and *education* have both been dichotomized. Those with a net monthly family income of less than € 2,000 are coded as "low income" and those with a net monthly family income of € 2,000 or more as "high income." Those who have not completed secondary education have been coded as "low level of education" and all others as "high level of education."

Age refers to respondent's age in years at the time of the survey.

Table 7.1
Factor Analysis of Items Indicating Economic Egalitarianism and Aversion to the Welfare State (no rotation)

Items	Factor 1	Factor 2
The welfare state makes people lazy.	0.46	0.59
Because of the welfare state, people don't care for each other anymore.	0.53	0.33
Nobody deserves a social security benefit, everybody should take care of him/herself.	0.08	0.62
Because of the welfare state, people no longer take care of themselves.	0.51	0.54
Only people who don't deserve it receive social security benefits.	0.43	0.45
Government should redistribute income in favour of the poor.	0.51	-0.44
In Flanders, big bosses make money at the expense of the workers.	0.66	-0.45
In Flanders, there is a law for the rich and there is a law for the poor.	0.72	-0.32
In Flanders, the rich get richer and the poor get poorer.	0.70	-0.31
Eigenvalue	2.65	1.92
R^2	0.29	0.21
Cronbach's α	0.69	0.53

Results

Economic Egalitarianism or Economic Populism?

The APS 1996 Survey contains a list of nine items, presumably intended by the data collectors to enable the construction of a "balanced" or "bipolar" one-dimensional measure of economic egalitarianism/conservatism. Five of these items refer to a rejection of the welfare state and are supposed to indicate economic conservatism (i.e., the upper five items in Table 7.1). Four others refer to resentment against social inequality and a desire for income redistribution and are supposed to indicate economic egalitarianism (i.e., the lower four items in Table 7.1).

A factor analysis of these nine items does however not produce the single one-dimensional and bipolar solution expected by the researchers, as Table 7.1 makes clear. First of all, not one, but two factors with an eigenvalue higher than one emerge, accounting for more than 50 percent of the total variance. Second, and even more striking, the expected bipolar economic egalitarianism/conservatism dimension is not even the strongest factor to emerge. It is after all clearly not the first, but the *second* factor that can be interpreted as such, because it combines positive loadings for the items expressing aversion to the welfare state with negative ones for those expressing resentment against social inequality and a desire for income redistribution. High scores on this second factor thus reflect economic conservatism and low ones economic egalitarianism.

The dominant first factor, explaining almost 30 percent of the total variance, shows positive loadings for all nine items, indicating a tendency of economic egalitarianism to go together with aversion to (rather than support for) the welfare state. Needless to say, then, this first and dominant factor cannot be interpreted as the classical divide between economic egalitarianism and economic conservatism, but should instead be interpreted as economic populism as it has been discussed above. As this is the strongest factor to emerge, it is of course not surprising that it is more reliable (Cronbach's $\alpha=0.69$) than the second economic egalitarian factor (Cronbach's $\alpha=0.53$).

Rotating this factor solution—the standard procedure if more factors with an eigenvalue higher than one are obtained—obviously results in separate measures for economic egalitarianism/conservatism and aversion to the welfare state. It needs to be emphasized, however, that such a rotation would still leave us with two separate and by and large independent measures rather than the single bipolar measure for economic egalitarian/conservatism that the researchers appear to have intended and expected. Moreover, unlike in Chapter 6, we are not interested here in explaining aversion to the welfare state, but rather in mapping and explaining economic populism. We therefore refrain from rotating our factor solution and instead assign scores for economic populism by saving the first unrotated factor displayed in Table 7.1.

Explaining Economic Populism

Does the working class set itself apart from society's more privileged classes by a stronger endorsement of economic populism? Table 7.2 points out that, indeed, the skilled and unskilled working class, just like those with low incomes and low levels of education, endorse economic

Table 7.2
Economic Populism Explained by Class, Income, Education, and Age
(standardized regression coefficients)

Independent variables	Economic populism
Higher professionals (I)	-0.10***
Lower professionals (II)	-0.09**
Nonmanual workers (III)	-0.01
Petty bourgeoisie (IV)	-0.06*
Skilled manual workers (V/VI)	0.11***
Unskilled manual workers (VII)	0.07**
Other wage earners	0.02
Not gainfully employed[1]	0
Low income	0.11***
Low level of education	0.10**
Age	0.19***
Adjusted R^2	0.14***

*p<0.05; ** p<0.01; *** p<0.001
1. Reference category

populism, thus curiously combining economic egalitarianism with authoritarianism-driven aversion to the welfare state.

Precisely because of the unconventional combination of economic egalitarianism and authoritarianism, economic populism can be attributed to neither a weak economic position nor limited cultural capital alone. Although this is difficult to assess with education tapping into both, we can study whether economic populism, like authoritarianism, is driven by feelings of anomie, too (e.g., Roberts and Rokeach 1956, Srole 1957, McDill 1961, Lutterman and Middleton 1970, Eisinga and Scheepers 1989: 262).

We therefore add political distrust, defeatism, and utilitarian individualism to the regression analysis. Previous research has pointed out that these three scales strongly drive rightist-populist Vlaams Blok voting and are strongly related among themselves, too (Elchardus and Derks 1998, Derks 2000). For our purposes here, it is however important to point out the differences that exist despite their strong mutual relationships. Political distrust and defeatism both indicate *anomie*, conceived of as a general lack of trust in society and its institutions, that has long been known to be strongly related to authoritarianism. *Political distrust* refers to a lack of trust in the three major Flemish political institutions, i.e., government, political parties, and parliament. The three items together constitute a reliable scale (Cronbach's $\alpha=0.88$) and scale scores have been assigned by saving factor scores. *Defeatism* refers to a gloomy (rather than optimistic) image of the future. Two items that exemplify the four items that have been used are "Looking at the future, it is barely justifiable to bring children into the world" and "Altogether I have faith in the future." These four items also constitute a reliable scale (Cronbach's $\alpha=0.71$) and scale scores have again been assigned as factor scores.

Utilitarian individualism needs to be distinguished from the two other measures of anomie, because it not only taps into the latter, but also into the more clearly ideological domain of *laissez-faire* liberalism that is not typically associated with the working class, being a discourse that emphasizes the primacy of individual survival and self-interest (Bellah et al. 1985). Two examples of the four items that have been used for its measurement are "Humanity, brotherhood, solidarity—all nonsense: Everybody has to take care of himself first and defend his own interest" and "What counts is money and power, the rest is just hot air." The four items that have been used to measure utilitarian individualism constitute a reliable scale (Cronbach's $\alpha=0.76$) and factor scores have been used to assign scale scores.

Table 7.3 adds political distrust, defeatism, and utilitarian individualism as additional independent variables to those that were already included in Table 7.2. It is clear that the previously recorded effects of class, income, and education become hardly weaker, while the two more valid measures of anomie, unlike more ideological utilitarian individualism, quite strongly lead to economic populism. This confirms that economic populism, like authoritarianism, is quite strongly affected by anomie, while it can simultaneously, like economic egalitarianism, be attributed to a weak economic position.

Progressive Working-Class Economic Egalitarianism?

The prevalence of economic populism among the working class suggests that working-class economic egalitarianism remains strongly particularistic, exclusionary, and self-serving. Could it be the case, then, that although economic egalitarianism is more widespread among the working class, as the class theory of politics has been assuming all along

Table 7.3
Economic Populism Explained by Class, Income, Education, Age, Anomie, and Utilitarian Individualism (standardized regression coefficients)

Independent variables	Economic populism
Higher professionals (I)	-0.10***
Lower professionals (II)	-0.08**
Nonmanual workers (III)	0.00
Petty bourgeoisie (IV)	-0.06*
Skilled manual workers (V/VI)	0.10***
Unskilled manual workers (VII)	0.05*
Other wage earners	0.01
Not gainfully employed[1]	0
Low income	0.07*
Low level of education	0.07*
Age	0.15***
Defeatism (anomie)	0.22***
Political distrust (anomie)	0.13***
Utilitarian individualism	0.05*
Adjusted R^2	0.22***

$p<0.05$; ** $p<0.01$; *** $p<0.001$
1. Reference category

and as our analyses have confirmed, it is yet more firmly embedded in a universalistic and inclusive progressive ideology among the middle class? To find out whether such is, indeed, the case, we finally analyze data from six countries from the first round of the *European Social Survey* (ESS 2002, edition 5.1) in which considerable proportions of the electorate vote for new rightist-populist parties nowadays: Austria (N=2,257); Denmark (N=1,506), France (N=1,503), Norway (N=2,036), Switzerland (N=2,040) and Flanders (N=1,234).[3]

We distinguish three different indicators for political progressiveness to find out whether they are more strongly related to economic egalitarianism[4] among the well educated than among the poorly educated:

authoritarianism/libertarianism,[5] left-right political self-identification,[6] and welfare chauvinism/universalism (a desire to exclude people from poor third-world countries from the national welfare system ("welfare chauvinism") or a willingness to share the wealth of the nation with them ("welfare universalism")).[7] Table 7.4 points out that libertarianism and welfare universalism are strongly and positively related among themselves, but only very weakly to economic egalitarianism. Economic egalitarianism, libertarianism, and welfare universalism are strongly and negatively related to rightist political self-identifications. None of this is surprising, because it is well known that the left-right distinction captures economic as well as cultural values, while these two types of values are almost unrelated among themselves among the public at large.

Does economic egalitarianism tend to go along with political conservatism among the poorly educated, while it is accompanied by political progressiveness among the well educated? To find out whether such is the case, we model the effects of education, the three indicators for political progressiveness, as well as interactions between the former and the latter on economic egalitarianism by means of multilevel analysis (Mixed models, SPSS), treating the individual level as nested in the country level.

Table 7.5 estimates the effects of welfare universalism and education. As the above would lead us to expect, the well educated are less economically egalitarian than those with a low or average level of education. Welfare universalism is positively related to economic egalitarianism, but the significant interactions between welfare universalism and education point out that this relationship is weaker among those with a low level of education. Progressive welfare universalism, in short, is more strongly related to economic egalitarianism among the well educated.

Table 7.4
Pearson's Correlations
(pairwise deletion, 8,426<N<10,465)

Variables	1	2	3	4
1. Welfare universalism	1.00			
2. Libertarianism	0.60***	1.00		
3. Rightist self-identification	-0.28***	-0.28***	1.00	
4. Economic egalitarianism	0.11***	0.07***	-0.29***	1.00***

*** $p<0.001$

Table 7.5
Economic Egalitarianism Explained by Welfare Universalism and Education
(multilevel analysis, N=8,349)

Independent variables	Estimate	Std. Error	t
Intercept	42.46	2.922***	14.53
Low level of education	25.93	1.929***	13.44
Medium level of education	20.70	1.706***	12.14
High level of education[1]	0		
Welfare universalism	0.38	0.027***	14.39
Welfare universalism x low education	-0.27	0.038***	-7.25
Welfare universalism x medium education	-0.26	0.031***	-8.60
Welfare universalism x high education[1]	0		
-2 Restricted log likelihood			80,474.66
Intraclass correlation (country)			0.08

* $p<0.05$; ** $p<0.01$; *** $p<0.001$
1. Reference category

Table 7.6 estimates the effects of authoritarianism and education on economic egalitarianism, producing patterns of association that are by and large identical to those in Table 7.5. Libertarianism goes together with egalitarianism, but this relationship is weaker among those with a low level of education. Again, then, we find that economic egalitarianism is less strongly related to progressive political values among the poorly educated.

Finally, Table 7.7 estimates the effects of left-right self-identification and education on economic egalitarianism, pointing out that—obviously—those who identify with the left are generally more economically egalitarian. These political self-identifications even explain away the whole tendency towards economic egalitarianism among the lower educated (not shown in Table 7.7). More importantly, leftist self-identifications are more strongly related to economic egalitarianism among the well educated, pointing out once again that among those with a low level of education economic egalitarianism is less strongly related to a progressive political profile.

Table 7.6
Economic Egalitarianism Explained by Libertarianism and Education
(multilevel analysis, N=8,971)

Independent variables	Estimate	Std. Error	t
Intercept	42.24	3.020***	13.99
Low level of education	26.15	2.246***	11.64
Medium level of education	21.88	2.037***	10.74
High level of education[1]	0		
Libertarianism	0.32	0.028***	11.68
Libertarianism x low education	-0.23	0.036***	-6.33
Libertarianism x medium education	-0.25	0.031***	-7.93
Libertarianism x high education[1]	0		
-2 Restricted log likelihood			86,814.85
Intraclass correlation (country)			0.08

* $p<0.05$; ** $p<0.01$; *** $p<0.001$
1. Reference category

Conclusion

Even in the 1970s, working-class aversion to social inequality did not necessarily translate into adherence to a full-fledged leftist ideology that also included support for the welfare state. To account for the by then already remarkably weak relationship between the two, Middendorp (1978: 354) invoked the Marxian concept of "false consciousness," thus suggesting that the combination of economic egalitarianism and aversion to the welfare state is "ideologically inconsistent." It surely is, of course, when it is judged from the classical left-right divide in politics and its construction of economic egalitarianism as "left" and aversion to the welfare state as "right."

Judged from the rightist-populist ideology that has emerged all over Europe since the 1980s, however, there is nothing particularly "inconsistent" about this combination. Populism, after all, constructs the welfare state as a system of exploitation through which a parasitic class of welfare loafers and bureaucratic and political elites infringes the economic rights of the common people. Even though it is a "thin" rather than a full-fledged ideology, then, there is nothing ideologically inconsistent about its endorsement of a desire for equality and simultaneous aversion to the welfare state.

Table 7.7
Economic Egalitarianism Explained by Rightist Self-Identification and Education (multilevel analysis, N=8,861)

Independent variables	Estimate	Std. Error	t
Intercept	86.12	2.531***	34.02
Low level of education	-3.47	1.615*	-2.15
Medium level of education	-4.35	1.324**	-3.29
High level of education[1]	0		
Rightist self-identification	-4.77	0.217***	-22.02
Rightist self-identification x low education	2.85	0.302***	9.41
Rightist self-identification x medium education	2.10	0.250***	8.40
Rightist self-identification x high education[1]	0		
-2 Restricted log likelihood			84,857.46
Intraclass correlation (country)			0.08

* p<0.05; ** p<0.01; *** p<0.001
1. Reference category

Indeed, the meaning of working-class economic egalitarianism differs radically from its middle-class counterpart. Among the middle class, where economic egalitarianism is less typical, it is nevertheless part and parcel of a progressive political outlook that includes an acceptance of cultural differences and post-traditional identities, a willingness to share the nation's wealth with immigrants from poor third-world countries, and leftist political self-identifications. Although economic egalitarianism is much more typical among the working class, it is more closely tied to authoritarian rejections of cultural diversity, desires to exclude immigrants from the national welfare system, and rightist political self-identifications there. Although economic egalitarianism is more typical of the working class, in short, it is more firmly embedded in a general progressive and inclusive political ideology in the middle class.

Notes

1. This claim is not just hot air, to be sure. Speaking of a *Matthew effect*, Deleeck (1977) has demonstrated already thirty years ago that the welfare state produces mechanisms that tend to lead it to serve the well off better than the poor. Populist understanding of the welfare state gains further credibility by the latter's complex-

ity and opacity, themselves inevitable side effects of the transition from private charity to public rights-based care arrangements. Just like the transparency of the democratic system declines if citizens gain more influence on public policy—in Canovan's (2002: 28) words: "Empowerment undermines transparency"—the expansion of the welfare state after all tends to make it more opaque, too.

2. This survey has been administered annually since 1996, inspired by the European Commission's *Eurobarometer*, the British *Social and Community Planning Research* and regular surveys by the Dutch *Social and Cultural Planning Office*.

3. The data, the questionnaire, and an extensive technical report are available on the Internet (http://ess.nsd.uib.no). We selected only those Belgian respondents who live in the Flemish region with its successful rightist-populist party Vlaams Blok. When the survey was held, no such party with a substantial electorate existed in the Walloon region (Swyngedouw 1998) and because of the Belgian federal political structure, Walloon voters cannot vote for Vlaams Blok/Vlaams Belang—not even in national elections.

4. Economic egalitarianism/conservatism is measured by means of two Likert items with response categories ranging from "Agree strongly" to "Disagree strongly": "The government should take measures to reduce income differences" and "Employees need strong trade unions to protect their working conditions and wages" (see also Chapter 2). Pearson's correlations between these items range from 0.23 to 0.31 in the six countries and scale scores have been assigned so as to range from 0 to 100, with high scores indicating economic egalitarianism and low ones economic conservatism.

5. Authoritarianism/libertarianism measures acceptance or rejection of cultural diversity. It is based on two Likert items expressing acceptance of cultural diversity ("Gay men and lesbians should be free to live their own life as they wish" and "It is better for a country if there are a variety of different religions") and two expressing its rejection ("It is better for a country if almost everyone shares the same customs and traditions" and "If a country wants to reduce tensions it should stop immigration"). Scale scores range from 0 to 100 with high scores indicating libertarianism and low ones authoritarianism.

6. Left-right political self-identification has been measured by asking respondents to place themselves on a scale ranging from 0 ("left") to 10 ("right").

7. Welfare chauvinism/universalism is measured by means of a series of five questions about support for strict or lenient immigration and asylum policies, mainly from an economic perspective: 1) "Most people who come to live here work and pay taxes. They also use health and welfare services. On balance, do you think people who come here take out more than they put in or put in more than they can take out?" (eleven response categories ranging between these two extremes). The second and third questions are Likert items with five response categories ranging from "Agree strongly" to "Disagree strongly": "(Respondent's country) has more than its fair share of people applying for refugee status" and "The government should be generous in judging people's applications for refugee status." The two final questions address the treatment of "People of a different race or ethnic group" and "People from the poorer countries outside Europe" preferred by the respondent (response categories: "Allow many to come and live here," "Allow some," "Allow a few," and "Allow none"). Scale scores range from 0 to 100 with low scores indicating welfare chauvinism and high ones welfare universalism.

8

Conclusion
Class Is Not Dead—It Has Been Buried Alive

No one suspected (...) or had reason to suspect, that she was not actually dead. She presented all the ordinary appearances of death. (...) The funeral (...) was hastened, on account of the rapid advance of what was supposed to be decomposition (Edgar Allan Poe, The Premature Burial, *1990 [1844]: 309).*

Introduction

Authors such as Inglehart (1977, 1990, 1997), Clark (1998, 2001a, Rempel and Clark 1997), and Hechter (2004) have claimed that we have been witnessing the emergence of a new political culture since World War II, which has gradually undermined class politics. Our findings point out that this is only partly true. Yes, we have been witnessing the emergence of a new political culture in which cultural issues pertaining to individual liberty and maintenance of social order have moved center stage. But no, there are hardly any indications that this has led to a decline of class politics. Increased rightist voting by the working class and limited working-class support for the welfare state are not caused by a decline of class politics, but by a dramatic proliferation of cultural politics. In this final chapter, we summarize the findings that lead us to these conclusions and elaborate on their theoretical implications.

Research Findings

We started in Chapter 2 with an exploration of why today so many workers vote for parties that contradict their class-based economic interests. Rightist voting by the working class proves to stem from a high level of authoritarianism that is rooted in limited cultural capital rather than in a weak economic position. Leftist voting by the working class can very well be explained by the class theory of politics, however: its weak economic position engenders working-class economic egalitarianism that drives leftist voting. As a consequence, the virtually absent relationship between class and voting in the Netherlands is the aggregated outcome of class voting for old-leftist and old-rightist parties and cross-cutting cultural voting for new-leftist and new-rightist parties. This means that the common practice since Alford's work in the 1960s is flawed: an absent relationship between class and voting does not necessarily indicate that class voting is absent.

In Chapter 3 we studied whether class voting and cultural voting depend on issue salience and whether the latter has changed in the United States during the period 1960-2000. Although cultural issues prove to have become more salient and cultural voting is stronger if cultural issues are salient, class issues have retained their salience and class voting proves remarkably immune to shifts in issue salience. While in Chapter 2 we had already concluded that class voting has not disappeared in the Netherlands, we thus again fail to find evidence for a decline of class politics in this chapter.

Reporting an analysis of the contents of party manifestos from twenty Western countries since World War II, Chapter 4 then demonstrated that the increased salience of cultural issues in the United States applies to the Western world generally. Cultural issues pertaining to individual liberty and social order have indeed become more salient, just like party polarization with respect to those issues. Although there has thus been a shift away from a political culture that revolves around class issues towards one in which cultural issues are central this does, again, not mean that class issues have become less salient since World War II. Although it is abundantly clear that cultural politics has become more widespread, then, we again find no clear evidence of a decline of class politics, raising doubts about whether the erosion of the alignment of the working class with the leftist parties really indicates a decline of class voting.

To find this out, we interrogated the validity of this familiar interpretation in Chapter 5 by means of a re-analysis of Nieuwbeerta's extremely large dataset, covering developments in no less than fifteen Western countries since the 1950s. Applying a careful distinction between class voting and cultural voting, our analyses indicate that the erosion of the alignment of the working class with the left since World War II denotes an increase of cultural voting rather than a decline of class voting.

Now that due to the rise of the new political culture moral notions of deservingness have become central to the debate about the welfare state, Chapter 6 demonstrates, economic egalitarianism can no longer simply be equated with solidarity with the unemployed. Consistent with the class theory of politics, to be sure, working-class economic egalitarianism fosters an emphasis on the right to social security and a preference for severing the link between work and income. This working-class solidarity with the unemployed is undermined by its cultural-capital based authoritarianism, however, which leads it to emphasize the obligation to work and strict notions of deservingness. As a consequence of these two cross-cutting tendencies, the working class is more economically egalitarian than society's other classes, yet not more strongly supportive of the welfare state.

Chapter 7 then focuses on countries in which, judged from the electoral successes of new-rightist populist parties, right-authoritarian issues have become highly salient. We demonstrate that in these political cultures economic egalitarianism and support for the welfare state have not simply grown apart, as Chapter 6 has demonstrated, but even tend to become mutually exclusive. The "economic populism" this produces, characterized by a remarkable combination of (leftist) economic egalitarianism and (rightist) aversion to the welfare state, is not only produced by a vulnerable economic position, but—just like authoritarianism—by feelings of anomie, too. And indeed, although economic egalitarianism, consistent with the class theory of politics, is more typical of the working class, it tends to remain exclusionary, particularistic, and self-serving there. While less typical of the middle class, it is more solidly embedded in a universalistic and inclusive progressive political ideology there. Even though the new political culture does not directly undermine working-class economic egalitarianism, then, it nevertheless tends to erode its wider ideological meaning and significance.

Class Is Not Dead—It Has Been Buried Alive

Our findings point out that, contrary to how they have typically been interpreted, the rightist tendencies among the working class that we have discussed in this book do not signify a decline of class politics. Class is not dead, but has been buried alive under the increasing weight of cultural politics.

Had political sociologists not relied so strongly and one-sidedly on the class theory of politics, the specter of the rightist working class would not even have appeared in the first place. Precisely because of its virtual theoretical monopoly, after all, the rightist working class has come to be construed as contradicting the class theory of politics and hence transformed into a hard-to-dispel specter. As we have seen, however, the rightist working class does in fact not so much contradict the class theory of politics, but rather confirms a cultural theory of politics.

The specter of the rightist working class was the well-deserved by-product of the theoretical narrow-mindedness of all those political sociologists who have been overly loyal to the class theory of politics. And yet, as a lamentable consequence of this theoretical complacency, poor old class now suffers its undeserved and horrid fate, buried alive "with thoughts of the air and grass above, with memory of dear friends who would fly to save us if but informed of our fate, and with consciousness that of this fate they can never be informed" (Poe 1990 [1844]: 312). To salvage it from this "most terrific of the ghastly extremes of agony" (Ibid.: 308) the specter of the rightist working class needs to be dispelled once and for all by breaking up the virtual theoretical monopoly of the class theory of politics and giving a cultural explanation its due, so as to more carefully disentangle class politics and cultural politics in future research.

Modernity and Its Discontents:
The Rise of the New Political Culture

With the benefit of hindsight, it is not even surprising that cultural politics has moved center stage. Classical arguments in the sociologies of culture and religion predict precisely that issues of individual liberty and maintenance of social order will become more salient due to the cultural consequences of modernization. It is a mere commonplace, after all, that processes of secularization (Berger 1967, Wilson 1982), detraditionalization (Heelas 1995), and individualization (Beck and Beck-Gernsheim 2002) entail an erosion of the unquestioned legitimacy of traditional institutions and the moral values that underlie them. And indeed, the increased salience of cultural issues does not result from the increase of affluence, as Inglehart suggests, but from the decline of Christian religion and the traditional moral values that are closely related to it (Achterberg 2006: 57-70).[1]

Traditional moral values bound up with the Christian tradition, once overarching society as a sort of "sacred canopy" (Berger 1967), have given way to a situation in which the social world has lost much of its former taken-for-grantedness. Indeed, as Max Weber predicted already a century ago, the disenchantment of the Western world erodes pre-given structures of identity and meaning, so that to an increasing extent "the world's processes (...) simply 'are' and 'happen' but no longer signify anything" (Weber 1978 [1921]: 506). In the words of Berger et al. (1973: 17-19), who argue that modernity creates a condition of "cultural homelessness": "The typical situation in which the individual finds himself in a traditional society is one where there are highly reliable plausibility structures. Conversely, modern societies are characterized by unstable, incohesive, unreliable plausibility structures. Put differently, in the modern situation certainty is hard to come by."

Detraditionalization creates problems of meaning and identity, in other words, more specifically the two principal "maladies of modernity": anomie and alienation (Zijderveld 2000: 199-201). Whereas alienation refers to a sort of "social claustrophobia" that fosters a desire to escape from a social system which forces one into "unnatural" social roles, anomie refers to a sort of "social agoraphobia," fostering a longing for re-establishing a predictable, safe, and familiar social world. Alienation thus underlies left-libertarian quests for individual liberty and self-attainment (Roszak 1969, Zijderveld 1970), while anomie drives right-authoritarian desires for re-establishing social order (e.g., Roberts and Rokeach 1956, McDill 1961, Blank 2003). Because traditional moral values have since World War II increasingly lost their former taken-for-grantedness, issues of individual liberty and social order have become increasingly important sources of cultural and political conflict, in short.

Historically speaking, traditional moral values first gave way to an "expressive" type of individualism (Bellah et al. 1985), referred to as "postmaterialism" by Inglehart (1977). Since they first became politically manifest on a large scale in the counter culture of the 1960s and 1970s and the left-libertarian social movements it spawned (Roszak 1969, Zijderveld 1970), these values have become increasingly widespread. Right-authoritarian desires for re-establishing social order were also already present in the heyday of the 1960s, when the countercultural political revolt met with working-class protest (Ransford 1972) and when polarization between libertarian and authoritarian students existed (Lyons 1996, Klatch 1999). While they remained more or less marginal and politically unorganized phenomena back then, "everything changed in the 1980s. New parties emerged, older ones radically innovated themselves, and both gained unprecedented consent" (Ignazi 2003: 1). Many European democracies witnessed the rise of new-rightist and populist parties that won considerable shares of the vote from the 1980s onwards (Veugelers 2000, Ignazi 1992, 2003).

Although Inglehart's (1977) influential analysis of the left-libertarian "silent revolution" and of "new politics" as essentially "left-libertarian politics" thus adequately represented the political climate in the 1960s and 1970s, the coexistence of new-leftist and new-rightist politics since the 1980s is difficult to reconcile with his theory of a gradually unfolding left-libertarian political culture. He has suggested in his book *The Silent Revolution*, for instance, that the Flemish and Walloon nationalists actually "represent the Left instead of the Right" (1977: 239), because they are also concerned with cultural rather than economic issues and because they also aim for social change. It has become abundantly clear since, however, that those are rightist movements that cannot be construed as support for his theory. More recently, reacting to his critic Ignazi (1992, 2003) who mockingly refers to the emergence of new rightist movements as a "silent counter-revolution," Inglehart has changed his position and now argues that "new rightist groups are a reaction against broader trends that are moving faster than these societies can assimilate them" (Inglehart 1997: 251).

Although he maintains confidently that these rightist reactions "do not represent the wave of the future" (1997: 251), Inglehart offers no clear reasons why this should be so. Why would right-authoritarian politics not simply be here to stay and grow? Indeed, if our analysis in this book is anything to go by, the Western democracies are likely to be witnessing neither a decline of class politics, nor an increase of the type of left-libertarian cultural politics emphasized in Inglehart's work. Making predictions is a tricky business, of course: *pace* Marx, capitalism is more vibrant than ever today, and *pace* Bell, an end of ideology hardly seems in sight. But even with the risk of being way off, we consider increasing conflict about cultural issues pertaining to individual liberty and social order a much more likely future for the western democracies than either a decline of class conflict or the emergence of a progressive left-libertarian consensus.

Note

1. For empirical studies of secularization and detraditionalization, the reader is referred to Houtman and Mascini (2002), Houtman (2003: 83-102), and Houtman and Aupers (2007).

Appendix 1: Measurement of Four Types of Issue Salience

Issue	Item #	Description
Controlled economy	per412	General need for direct government control of economy; control over prices, wages, rents, etc.; state intervention into the economic system.
Economic planning	per404	Favorable mentions of long-standing economic planning of a consultative or indicative nature, need for government to create such a plan.
Nationalization	per413	Favorable mentions of government ownership, partial or complete, including government ownership of land.
Welfare state expansion	per504	Favorable mentions of need to introduce, maintain or expand any social service or social security scheme; support for social services such as health service or social housing.
Free enterprise	per401	Favorable mentions of free enterprise capitalism; superiority of individual enterprise over state and control systems; favorable mentions of private property rights, personal enterprise and initiative; need for unhampered individual enterprise.
Economic incentives	per402	Need for wage and tax policies to induce enterprise; encouragement to start enterprises; need for financial and other incentives such as subsidies.
Economic orthodoxy	per414	Need for traditional economic orthodoxy, e.g., reduction of budget deficits, retrenchment in crisis, thrift and savings; support for traditional economic institutions such as stock market and banking system; support for strong currency.
Welfare state limitation	per505	Limiting expenditure on social services or social security; otherwise as "welfare state expansion," but negative.

Appendix 1 (cont.)

National way of life positive	per601	Appeals to patriotism and/or nationalism; suspension of some freedoms in order to protect the state against subversion; support for established national ideas.
Traditional morality positive	per603	Favorable mentions of traditional moral values; prohibition censorship and suppression of immorality and unseemly behavior; maintenance and stability of family; religion.
Law and order	per605	Enforcement of all laws; actions against crime; support and resources for police; tougher attitudes in courts.
National way of life negative	per602	Against patriotism and/or nationalism; opposition to the existing national state; otherwise as "national way of life positive," but negative.
Traditional morality negative	per604	Opposition to traditional moral values; support for divorce, abortion, etc.; otherwise as "traditional morality positive," but negative.
Underprivileged minority groups	per705	Favorable mentions to underprivileged minorities who are defined neither in economic nor in demographic terms, e.g. the handicapped, disabled, homosexuals, immigrants, refugees etc.

Source: Budge et al. (2001: 222-228).

Appendix 2: Secondary Data Sources

Budge, Ian, Hans-Dieter Klingemann, Andrea Volkens, Judith Bara, and Eric Tanenbaum, *Manifesto Dataset*, CD-ROM delivered with the book *Mapping Policy Preferences: Estimates for Parties, Electors, and Governments 1945-1998*, 2001, New York: Oxford University Press.

Department of the Flemish Community, APS Survey: Sociaal-culturele verschuivingen in Vlaanderen, 1996 [*APS Survey: Socio-Cultural Shifts in Flanders, 1996*], Brussels: Department of the Flemish Community.

Jowell, Roger, and central coordinating team, *European Social Survey 2002*, London: Centre for Comparative Social Surveys, City University.

Nieuwbeerta, Paul, and Harry Ganzeboom, *International Social Mobility and Politics File: Documentation of an Integrated Dataset of 113 National Surveys Held in 16 countries, 1956-1991*, Amsterdam: Steinmetz Archive / SWIDOC, serial number P1145.

Sapiro, Virginia, Steven J. Rosenstone, *American National Election Studies Cumulative Data File, 1948-2000*, University of Michigan, Center for Political Studies [producer] / Inter-university Consortium for Political and Social Research [distributor], MI: Ann Arbor, 11th ICPSR version.

The original data creators or those who carried out the original collection of the data, the depositors, and the funders of the data collections, bear no responsibility for the analysis or interpretation of those data in this book.

References

Abramson, Paul R. and Ronald Inglehart. 1995. *Value Change in Global Perspective*. Ann Arbor, MI: University of Michigan Press.

Achterberg, Peter. 2006. *Considering Cultural Conflict: Class Politics and Cultural Politics in Western Societies*. Maastricht: Shaker.

Adorno, Theodor W., Else Frenkel Brunswik, Daniel J. Levinson, and R. Nevitt Sandford. 1950. *The Authoritarian Personality*. New York: Harper and Row.

Alford, Robert R. 1967. "Class Voting in the Anglo-American Political Systems." Pp. 67-93 in *Party Systems and Voter Alignments: Cross-National Perspectives*, edited by Seymour Martin Lipset and Stein Rokkan. New York: Free Press.

Andersen, Jørgen Goul. 1992. "Denmark: The Progress Party—Populist Neo-Liberalism and Welfare State Chauvinism." Pp. 193-205 in *The Extreme Right in Europe and the USA*, edited by Paul Hainsworth. London: Pinter.

Andersen, Robert and Anthony Heath. 2002. "Class Matters: The Persisting Effects of Contextual Social Class on Individual Voting in Britain, 1964-97." *European Sociological Review* 18:125-138.

Baker, Kendall L., Russel J. Dalton, and Kai Hildebrandt. 1981. *Germany Transformed: Political Culture and the New Politics*. Cambridge, MA: Harvard University Press.

Bakker, Bart, Inge Sieben, Paul Nieuwbeerta, and Harry Ganzeboom. 1997. "Maten voor prestige, sociaal-economische status en sociale klasse voor de standaard beroepen classificatie 1992" [Measures for Prestige, Socio-Economic Status, and Social Class for the Standard Occupational Classification 1992]. *Sociale Wetenschappen* 40:1-22.

Beck, Ulrich and Elisabeth Beck-Gernsheim. 2002. *Individualization: Institutionalized Individualism and Its Social and Political Consequences*. London: Sage.

Bell, Daniel. 1980. "The New Class: A Muddled Concept." Pp. 144-164 in *The Winding Passage: Essays and Sociological Journeys, 1960-1980*, by Daniel Bell. Cambridge, MA: ABT.

Bellah, Robert N., William M. Sullivan, Steven M. Tipton, Ann Swindler, and Richard Madsen. 1985. *Habits of the Heart: Individualism and Commitment in American Life*. Berkeley: University of California Press.

Benn, Stanley I. and Richard S. Peters. 1977. *Social Principles and the Democratic State*. London: Allen and Unwin.

Berger, Peter L. 1967. *The Sacred Canopy: Elements of a Sociology of Religion*. New York: Doubleday.

Berger, Peter L., Brigitte Berger, and Hansfried Kellner. 1973. *The Homeless Mind: Modernization and Consciousness*. Random House: New York.

Betz, Hans-Georg. 1994. *Radical Right-Wing Populism in Western Europe*. New York: St. Martin's Press.

Blank, Thomas. 2003. "Determinants of National Identity in East and West Germany: An Empirical Comparison of Theories on the Significance of Authoritarianism, Anomie, and General Self-Esteem." *Political Psychology* 24:259-288.

Bobbio, Norbert. 1996. *Left and Right: The Significance of a Political Distinction*. Cambridge: Polity Press.

Bourdieu, Pierre. 1984. *Distinction: A Social Critique of the Judgement of Taste.* London: Routledge and Kegan Paul.

Bourdieu, Pierre. 1986. "The Forms of Capital." Pp. 241-258 in *Handbook of Theory and Research for the Sociology of Education,* edited by John G. Richardson. New York: Greenwood Press.

Brint, Steven. 1984. "'New-Class and Cumulative Trend Explanations of the Liberal Political Attitudes of Professionals." *American Journal of Sociology* 90:30-71.

Brooks, Clem, Paul Nieuwbeerta, and Jeff Manza. 2006. "Cleavage-Based Voting Behavior in Cross-National Perspective: Evidence From Six Postwar Democracies." *Social Science Research* 35:88-128.

Bruce-Briggs, Barry (Ed.). 1979. *The New Class?* New Brunswick, N.J.: Transaction Publishers.

Buchanan, Allen and Deborah Mathieu. 1986. "Philosophy and Justice." Pp. 11-45 in *Justice: Views from the Social Sciences,* edited by Ronald L. Cohen. New York: Plenum.

Budge, Ian. 2000. "Expert Judgements of Party Policy Positions: Uses and Limitations in Political Research." *European Journal of Political Research* 37:103-113.

Budge, Ian, and Hans-Dieter Klingemann. 2001. "Finally! Comparative Over-Time Mapping of Party Policy Movement." Pp. 19-50 in *Mapping Policy Preferences: Estimates for Parties, Electors, and Governments 1945-1998,* edited by Ian Budge, Andrea Volkens, Judith Bara, and Eric Tanenbaum. Oxford: Oxford University Press.

Budge, Ian, Dave Robertson, and Derek J. Hearl (Eds). 1987. *Ideology, Strategy and Party Change: Spatial Analysis of Post-War Election Programmes in 19 Democracies.* Cambridge: Cambridge University Press.

Budge, Ian, Andrea Volkens, Judith Bara, and Eric Tanenbaum (Eds). 2001. *Mapping Policy Preferences: Estimates for Parties, Electors, and Governments 1945-1998.* Oxford: Oxford University Press.

Canovan, Margaret. 2002. "Taking Politics to the People: Populism as the Ideology of Democracy." Pp. 25-44 in *Democracies and the Populist Challenge,* edited by Yves Mény and Yves Surel. Houndmills: Palgrave.

Carmines, Edward G. and Geoffrey C. Layman. 1997. "Value Priorities, Partisanship, and Electoral Choice: The Neglected Case of the United States." *Political Behavior* 19:283-316.

Clark, Terry Nichols. 1998. "Assessing the New Political Culture by Comparing Cities Around the World." Pp. 93-194 in *The New Political Culture,* edited by Terry Nichols Clark and Vincent Hoffman-Martinot. Boulder, CO: Westview Press.

Clark, Terry Nichols. 2001a. "What Have We Learned in a Decade on Class and Party Politics?" Pp. 6-39 in *The Breakdown of Class Politics: A Debate on Post-Industrial Stratification,* edited by Terry Nichols Clark and Seymour Martin Lipset. Baltimore, MD: Johns Hopkins University Press.

Clark, Terry Nichols. 2001b. "The Debate over 'Are Social Classes Dying?'" Pp. 273-319 in *The Breakdown of Class Politics: A Debate on Post-Industrial Stratification,* edited by Terry Nichols Clark and Seymour Martin Lipset. Baltimore, MD: Johns Hopkins University Press.

Clark, Terry Nichols and Seymour Martin Lipset. 1991. "Are Social Classes Dying?" *International Sociology* 6:397-410.

Clark, Terry Nichols and Seymour Martin Lipset (Eds). 2001. *The Breakdown of Class Politics: A Debate on Post-Industrial Stratification.* Baltimore, MD: Johns Hopkins University Press.

Cook, Karen S. and Karen A. Hegtvedt. 1983. "Distributive Justice, Equity, and Equality." *Annual Review of Sociology* 9:217-241.

Dalton, Russell J. 1988. *Citizen Politics in Western Democracies: Public Opinion and Political Parties in the United States, Great Britain, Germany, and France.* Catham: House Publishers Catham.
Dalton, Russel J., Scott C. Flanagan, and Paul Allen Beck. 1984. Elecoral Change in Advanced Industrial Democracies: Realignment or Dealignment? Princeton NJ: Princeton University Press.
De Benoist, Alain. 1995. "End of the Left-Right Dichotomy: The French Case." *Telos* 27:73-90.
De Graaf, Nan Dirk and Bram Steijn. 1997. "De 'service' klasse in Nederland: Een voorstel tot aanpassing van de EGP-klassenindeling" [The Service Class in the Netherlands: A Proposal to Adjust the EGP Class Schema]. *Tijdschrift voor Sociologie* 18:131-154.
De Graaf, Nan Dirk, Anthony F. Heath, and Ariana Need. 2001. "Declining Cleavages and Political Choices: The Interplay of Social and Political Factors in the Netherlands." *Electoral Studies* 20:1-15.
De Graaf, Paul M. and Matthijs Kalmijn. 2001. "Trends in the Intergenerational Transmission of Cultural and Economic Status." *Acta Sociologica* 44:51-66.
Dekker, Paul and Peter Ester. 1987. "Working Class Authoritarianism: A Re-Examination of the Lipset Thesis." *European Journal of Political Research* 15:395-415.
Dekker, Paul and Peter Ester. 1993. *Social and Political Attitudes in Dutch Society.* Rijswijk: SCP.
Dekker, Paul, Peter Ester, and Andries Van den Broek. 1999. "Fixing Left and Right: Value Orientations According to Middendorp and Inglehart." Pp. 151-176 in *Ideology in the Low Countries, Trends, Models and Lacunae,* edited by Hans De Witte and Peer Scheepers. Assen: Van Gorcum.
Deleeck, Herman. 1977. *Ongelijkheden in de welvaartsstaat* [Inequalities in the Welfare State]. Antwerpen: De Nederlandsche Boekhandel.
Derks, Anton. 2000. *Individualisme zonder verhaal: Een onderzoek naar de verspreiding en de betekenis van individualistische vertogen in Vlaanderen* [Individualism Without a Cause: A Study into the Distribution and Meaning of Individualist Discourses in Flanders]. Brussel: Vubpress.
De Witte, Hans. 1990. *Conformisme, radicalisme en machteloosheid: Een onderzoek naar de sociaal-culturele en sociaal-economische opvattingen van arbeiders in Vlaanderen* [Conformism, Radicalism, and Powerlessness: A Study of the Socio-Cultural and Socio-Economic Attitudes of Workers in Flanders]. Leuven: HIVA.
De Witte, Hans and Jaak Billiet. 1999. "Economic and Cultural Conservatism in Flanders: In Search of Concepts, Determinants and Impact on Voting Behaviour." Pp. 91-120 in *Ideology in the Low Countries: Trends, Models and Lacunae,* edited by Hans De Witte and Peer Scheepers. Assen: Van Gorcum.
DiMaggio, Paul. 1982. "Cultural Capital and School Success: The Impact of Status Culture Participation on the Grades of U.S. High School Students." *American Sociological Review* 47:189-201.
DiMaggio, Paul, John A. Evans, and Bethany Bryson. 1996. "Have Americans' Social Attitudes Become More Polarized?" Pp. 63-100 in *Culture Wars in American Politics: Critical Reviews of a Popular Myth,* edited by Rhys Williams. New York: Aldine de Gruyter.
DiMaggio, Paul and John Mohr. 1985. "Cultural Capital, Educational Attainment, and Marital Selection." *American Journal of Sociology* 90:1231-1261.
Di Tella, Torcuato S. 1995. "Populism." Pp. 985-989 in *The Encyclopedia of Democracy (Volume III),* edited by Seymour Martin Lipset. Washington D.C.: Congressional Quarterly Inc.

Dittrich, Boris. 2003. Retrieved 10 June 2005, from: *http://www.borisdittrich.nl/article. php?sid=190.*
Draulans, Veerle and Loek Halman. 2003. "Religious and Moral Pluralism in Contemporary Europe." Pp. 371-400 in *The Cultural Diversity of European Unity*, edited by Wil Arts, Jacques Hagenaars, and Loek Halman. Leiden: Brill.
Duncan, Otis Dudley. 1961. "A Socioeconomic Index for all Occupations." Pp. 109-138 in *Occupations and Social Status,* edited by Albert J. Reiss Jr. New York: Free Press.
Dunlap, Riley E. and Rik Scarce. 1991. "Poll Trends: Environmental Problems and Protection." *Public Opinion Quarterly* 55:651-672.
Edlund, Jonas. 1999. "Trust in Government and Welfare Regimes: Attitudes to Redistribution and Financial Cheating in the USA and Norway." *European Journal of Political Research* 35:341-370.
Eisinga, Rob and Peer Scheepers. 1989. *Etnocentrisme in Nederland: Theoretische en empirische verkenningen* [Ethnocentrism in the Netherlands: Theoretical and Empirical Explorations]. Nijmegen: ITS.
Elchardus, Mark. 1996. "Class, Cultural Re-Alignment and the Rise of the Populist Right." Pp. 41-63 in *Changing Europe: Some Aspects of Identity, Conflict and Social Justice*, edited by Agnus Erskine. Avebury: Aldershot.
Elchardus, Mark and Anton Derks. 1998. "Discourses about the Relationship Between the Individual and Society in Flanders: The Consequences of Individualistic Challenges in a Collectivistic Culture." *Ethical Perspectives* 5:109-126.
Erikson, Robert. 1984. "Social Class of Men, Women and Families." *Sociology* 18:500-514.
Erikson, Robert and John H. Goldthorpe. 1992. *The Constant Flux: A Study of Class Mobility in Industrial Societies.* Oxford: Clarendon Press.
Erikson, Robert, John H. Goldthorpe, and Lucienne Portocarero. 1979. "Intergenerational Class Mobility in Three Western European Countries." *British Journal of Sociology* 30:415-441.
Esping-Andersen, Gøsta. 1990. *The Three Worlds of Welfare Capitalism.* Cambridge: Polity Press.
Evans, Geoffrey (Ed.). 1999a. *The End of Class Politics? Class Voting in Comparative Context.* Oxford: Oxford University Press.
Evans, Geoffrey. 1999b. "Class Voting: From Premature Obituary to Reasoned Appraisal" Pp. 1-22 in *The End of Class Politics? Class Voting in Comparative Perspective*, edited by Geoffrey Evans. Oxford: Oxford University Press.
Evans, Geoffrey. 2000. "The Continued Significance of Class Voting." *Annual Review of Political Science* 3:401-417.
Evans, Geoffrey, Anthony Heath, and Mansur Lalljee. 1996. "Measuring Left-Right and Libertarian-Authoritarian Values in the British Electorate." *British Journal of Sociology* 47:93-112.
Evans, Geoffrey, Anthony Heath, and Clive Payne. 1999. "Class: Labour as a Catch-All Party?" Pp. 87-101 in *Critical Elections: British Parties and Voters in Long-Term Perspective*, edited by Geoffrey Evans and Pippa Norris. London: Sage.
Evans, John H. and Bethany Bryson. 2001. "Opinion Polarization: Important Contributions, Necessary Limitations." *American Journal of Sociology* 106:944-960.
Felling, Albert and Jan Peters. 1986. "Conservatism: A Multidimensional Concept." *Netherlands' Journal of Sociology* 22:36-60.
Flanagan, Scott C. 1979. "Value Change and Partisan Change in Japan: The Silent Revolution Revisited." *Comparative Politics* 11:253-278.
Flanagan, Scott C. 1982. "Changing Values in Advanced Industrial Societies: Inglehart's Silent Revolution from the Perspective of Japanese Findings." *Comparative Political Studies* 14:403-44.

Flanagan, Scott C. 1987. "Value Change in Industrial Societies: Reply to Inglehart." *American Political Science Review* 81:1303-1319.

Flanagan, Scott C. and Aie-Rie Lee. 2003. "The New Politics, Culture Wars, and the Authoritarian-Libertarian Value Change in Advanced Industrial Democracies." *Comparative Political Studies* 36:235-270.

Fleishman, John A. 1988. "Attitude Organization in the General Public: Evidence for a Bidimensional Structure." *Social Forces* 67:159-184.

Fournier, Patrick, Andre Blais, Richard Nadeau, Elizabeth Gidengil, and Neil Nevitte. 2003. "Issue Importance and Performance Voting." *Political Behavior* 25:51-67.

Franklin, Mark N. 1982. "Demographic and Political Components in the Decline of British Class Voting 1964-1979." *Electoral Studies* 1:195-220.

Franklin, Mark N. 1985. *The Decline of Class Voting in Britain: Changes in the Basis of Electoral Choice, 1964-1983.* Oxford: Clarendon Press.

Gabennesch, Howard. 1972. "Authoritarianism as World View." *American Journal of Sociology* 77:857-875.

Ganzeboom, Harry, and Donald Treiman. 2005. *International Stratification and Mobility File: Conversion Tools.* http://www.fsw.vu.nl/~h.ganzeboom/ismf 2005.

Geser, Hans. 1998. "Toward a One-Dimensional Ideological Culture? Evidence from Swiss Local Parties." Pp. 235-260 in *The New Political Culture*, edited by Terry Nichols Clark and Vincent Hoffman-Martinot. Boulder, CO: Westview Press.

Giddens, Anthony. 1994. *Beyond Left and Right: The Future of Radical Politics.* Cambridge: Polity Press.

Gilder, George. 1981. *Wealth and Poverty.* New York: Basic Books.

Goldthorpe, John H. 1980. *Social Mobility and Class Structure in Modern Britain.* Oxford: Clarendon Press.

Goldthorpe, John H., David Lockwood, Frank Bechhofer, and Jennifer Platt. 1969. *The Affluent Worker in the Class Structure.* Cambridge: Cambridge University Press.

Grabb, Edward G. 1979. "Working-Class Authoritarianism and Tolerance of Outgroups: A Reassessment." *Public Opinion Quarterly* 43:36-47.

Grabb, Edward G. 1980. "Marxist Categories and Theories of Class: The Case of Working Class Authoritarianism." *Pacific Sociological Review* 23:359-376.

Heath, Anthony F., Geoffrey Evans, and Jean Martin. 1994. "The Measurement of Core Beliefs and Values: The Development of Balanced Socialist/Laissez Faire and Libertarian/Authoritarian Scales." *British Journal of Political Science* 24:115-132.

Heath, Anthony F., Geoffrey Evans, and Clive Payne. 1995. "Modelling the Class-Party Relationship in Britain, 1964-92." *Journal of the Royal Statistical Society (Series A)* 158:563-574.

Heath, Anthony F., Roger M. Jowell, John Curtice, and Geoffrey Evans. 1990. "The Rise of the New Political Agenda?" *European Sociological Review* 6:31-48.

Heath, Anthony F., Michael Yang, and Harvey Goldstein. 1996. "Multilevel Analysis of the Changing Relationship Between Class and Party in Britain 1964-1992." *Quality and Quantity* 30:389-404.

Hechter, Michael. 2004. "From Class to Culture." *American Journal of Sociology* 110:400-445.

Heelas, Paul. 1995. "Introduction: Detraditionalization and Its Rivals." Pp. 1-20 in *Detraditionalization: Critical Reflections on Authority and Identity,* edited by Paul Heelas, Scott Lash, and Paul Morris. Oxford: Blackwell.

Higgins, Joan. 1981. *States of Welfare: Comparative Analysis in Social Policy.* Oxford: Basil Blackwell.

Hoffman-Martinot, Vincent. 1991. "Grüne and Verts: Two Faces of European Ecologism." *West European Politics* 14:70-95.

Horowitz, Irving Louis. 1977. "The Present Conditions of the American Working Class." Pp. 98-112 in *Ideology and Utopia in the United States, 1956-1976*, by Irving Louis Horowitz. New York: Oxford University Press.

Horowitz, Irving Louis. 1984. "Class Composition and Competition." Pp. 3-19 in *Winners and Losers: Social and Political Polarities in America*, by Irving Louis Horowitz. Durham, NC: Duke University Press.

Hout, Mike, Clem Brooks, and Jeff Manza. 1993. "The Persistence of Classes in Post-Industrial Societies." *International Sociology* 8:259-278.

Houtman, Dick. 1994. *Werkloosheid en sociale rechtvaardigheid: Oordelen over de rechten en plichten van werklozen* [Unemployment and Social Justice: Judgments on the Rights and Obligations of the Unemployed]. Amsterdam: Boom.

Houtman, Dick. 1997. "Welfare State, Unemployment, and Social Justice: Judgments on the Rights and Obligations of the Unemployed." *Social Justice Research* 10:267-288.

Houtman, Dick. 2001. "Class, Culture, and Conservatism: Reassessing Education as a Variable in Political Sociology." Pp. 161-195 in *The Breakdown of Class Politics: A Debate on Post-Industrial Stratification*, edited by Terry Nichols Clark and Seymour Martin Lipset. Baltimore, MD: Johns Hopkins University Press.

Houtman, Dick. 2003. *Class and Politics in Contemporary Social Science: "Marxism Lite" and Its Blind Spot for Culture*. New York: Aldine de Gruyter.

Houtman, Dick. 2004. "Lipset and 'Working-Class' Authoritarianism". Pp. 131-160 in *Civil Society and Class Politics: Essays on the Political Sociology of Seymour Martin Lipset*, edited by Irving Louis Horowitz. New Brunswick, NJ: Transaction.

Houtman, Dick, and Stef Aupers. 2007. "The Spiritual Turn and the Decline of Tradition: The Spread of Post-Christian Spirituality in Fourteen Western Countries (1981-2000)." *Journal for the Scientific Study of Religion* 46:305-320.

Houtman, Dick, and Peter Mascini. 2002. "Why Do Churches Become Empty, While New Age Grows? Secularization and Religious Change in the Netherlands." *Journal for the Scientific Study of Religion* 41:455-473.

Hunter, James D. 1991. *Culture Wars: The Struggle to Define America*. New York: Basic Books.

Ignazi, Piero. 1992. "The Silent Counter-Revolution: Hypotheses on the Emergence of Extreme Right-Wing Parties in Europe." *European Journal of Political Research* 22:3-34.

Ignazi, Piero. 2003. *Extreme Right Parties in Western Europe*. Oxford: Oxford University Press.

Inglehart, Ronald. 1977. *The Silent Revolution: Changing Values and Political Styles among Western Publics*. Princeton, NJ: Princeton University Press.

Inglehart, Ronald. 1987. "Value Change in Industrial Societies." *American Political Science Review* 81:1289-1303.

Inglehart, Ronald. 1990. *Culture Shift in Advanced Industrial Society*. Princeton, NJ: Princeton University Press.

Inglehart, Ronald. 1997. *Modernization and Postmodernization: Cultural, Economic, and Political Change in 43 Countries*. Princeton, NJ: Princeton University Press.

Inglehart, Ronald and Jacques-René Rabier. 1986. "Political Realignment in Advanced Industrial Society: From Class-Based Politics to Quality of Life Politics." *Government and Opposition* 21:456-479.

Ionescu, Ghita and Ernest Gellner (Eds). 1969. *Populism: Its Meaning and National Characteristics*. London: Weidenfeld and Nicolson.

Ishida, Hiroshi and Walter Muller. 1995. "Class Origin, Class Destination, and Education: A Cross-National Study of Ten Industrial Nations." *American Journal of Sociology* 101:145-194.

Jones, Catherina. 1985. *Patterns of Social Policy: An Introduction to Comparative Analysis*. London: Tavistock.
Kalmijn, Matthijs. 1994. "Assortative Mating by Cultural and Economic Occupational Status." *American Journal of Sociology* 100:422-452.
Kelly, K. Dennis and William J. Chambliss. 1966. "Status Consistency and Political Attitudes." *American Sociological Review* 31:375-382.
Kerr, Clark, John T. Dunlap, Frederick Harbison, and Charles A. Myers. 1960. *Industrialism and Industrial Man*. Cambridge, MA: Harvard University Press.
Kitschelt, Herbert. 1995. *The Radical Right in Western Europe: A Comparative Analysis*. Ann Arbor: University of Michigan Press.
Kitschelt, Herbert and Staf Hellemans. 1990. "The Left-Right Semantics and the New Politics Cleavage." *Comparative Political Studies* 23:210-238.
Klatch, Rebecca E. 1999. *A Generation Divided: The New Left, the New Right, and the 1960s*. Berkeley: University of California Press.
Knutsen, Oddbjorn. 1998. "Change in Party Positions: Comparing Expert Surveys." *West European Politics* 21:63-94.
Kochuyt, Thierry and Anton Derks. 2003. "Bitter als de brakke morgen: Over het ressentiment van ondergeschikte posities" [Bitter as the Brackish Morning: On the Resentment of Subordinate Positions]. *Amsterdams Sociologisch Tijdschrift* 30:463-497.
Kohn, Melvin L. 1977 [1969]. *Class and Conformity: A Study in Values (Second Edition)*. Chicago: University of Chicago Press.
Kohn, Melvin L. and Kazimierz M. Slomczynski. 1990. *Social Structure and Self-Direction: A Comparative Analysis of the United States and Poland*. Oxford: Basil Blackwell.
Korpi, Walter and Joakim Palme. 2003. "New Politics and Class Politics in the Context of Austerity and Globalization: Welfare State Regress in 18 Countries, 1975–95." *American Political Science Review* 97:425-446.
Kriesi, Hanspeter. 1989. "New Social Movements and the New Class in the Netherlands." *American Journal of Sociology* 94:1078-1116.
Kriesi, Hanspeter. 1998. "The Transformation of Cleavage Politics: The 1997 Stein Rokkan Lecture." *European Journal of Political Research* 33:165-185.
Kriesi, Hanspeter and Philip Van Praag. 1987. "Old and New Politics: The Dutch Peace Movement and the Traditional Political Organizations." *European Journal of Political Research* 15:319-346.
Lamont, Michèle. 1986. "Cultural Capital and the Liberal Political Attitudes of Professionals: Comment on Brint." *American Journal of Sociology* 92:1501-1506.
Lamont, Michèle. 2000. *The Dignity of Working Men: Morality and the Boundaries of Race, Class and Immigration*. Cambridge, MA: Harvard University Press.
Layman, Geoffrey C. 2001. *The Great Divide: Religious and Cultural Conflict in American Party Politics*. New York: Columbia University Press.
Layman, Geoffrey C. and Edward G. Carmines. 1997. "Cultural Conflict in American Politics: Religious Traditionalism, Postmaterialism, and U.S. Political Behavior." *Journal of Politics* 59:751-777.
Lazarsfeld, Paul F., Bernard Berelson, and Hazel Gaudet. 1972 [1944]. *The People's Choice: How the Voter Makes Up His Mind in a Presidential Campaign (Third Edition)*. New York: Columbia University Press.
Lenin, Vladimir Illyich. 1968 [1916]. "Imperialism: The Highest Stage of Capitalism." Pp. 169-262 in *Lenin: Selected Works*. Moscow: Progress.
Lipset, Seymour Martin. 1959. "Democracy and Working-Class Authoritarianism." *American Sociological Review* 24:482-502.
Lipset, Seymour Martin. 1960. *Political Man: The Social Bases of Politics*. New York: Doubleday.

Lipset, Seymour Martin. 1970. *Revolution and Counter-Revolution*. New York: Doubleday.
Lipset, Seymour Martin. 1981. *Political Man: The Social Bases of Politics (Expanded Edition)*. Baltimore, MD: Johns Hopkins University Press.
Lipset, Seymour Martin. 2001. "Cleavages, Parties and Democracy." Pp. 3-11 in *Party Systems and Voter Alignments Revisited*, edited by Lauri Karvonen and Stein Kuhnle. London: Routledge.
Lipset, Seymour Martin and Stein Rokkan (Eds). 1967. *Party Systems and Voter Alignments: Cross-National Perspectives*. New York: Free Press.
Lipsitz, Lewis. 1965. "Working-Class Authoritarianism: A Re-Evaluation." *American Sociological Review* 30:103-109.
Lis, Catharina and Hugo Soly. 1979. *Poverty and Capitalism in Pre-Industrial Europe*. Brighton: Harvester Press.
Lutterman, Kenneth G. and Russell Middleton. 1970. "Authoritarianism, Anomia, and Prejudice." *Social Forces* 48:485-492.
Lyons, Paul. 1996. *New Left, New Right and the Legacy of the Sixties*. Philadelphia: Temple University Press.
Macarov, David. 1980. *Work and Welfare: The Unholy Alliance*. Beverly Hills: Sage.
MacKenzie, Gavin. 1967. "The Economic Dimensions of Embourgeoisement." *British Journal of Sociology* 18: 29-44.
Manza, Jeff and Clem Brooks. 1996. "Does Class Analysis Still Have Anything to Contibute to the Study of Politics? Comments." *Theory and Society* 25:717-723.
Manza, Jeff and Clem Brooks. 1999. *Social Cleavages and Political Change: Voter Alignments and U.S. Party Coalitions*. Oxford/New York: Oxford University Press.
Marshall, Gordon, Howard Newby, David Rose, and Carolyn Vogler. 1988. *Social Class in Modern Britain*. London: Hutchinson.
Marshall, Thomas H. 1965. "Citizenship and Social Class." Pp. 71-134 in *Class, Citizenship and Social Development*, by Thomas H. Marshall. New York: Anchor Books.
Marx, Karl. 1963 [1852]. "The Chartists." Pp. 204-207 in *Karl Marx: Selected Writings in Sociology and Social Philosophy*, edited by Tom B. Bottomore and Maximilien Rubel. Harmondsworth: Penguin Books.
Marx, Karl. 1967 [1867]. *Capital: A Critique of Political Economy (Volume 1)*. New York: International Publishers.
Marx, Karl and Friedrich Engels. 1948 [1848]. *Manifesto of the Communist Party*. New York: International Publishers.
McAllister, Ian and Donley T. Studlar. 1995. "New Politics and Partisan Alignment: Values, Ideology and Elites in Australia." *Party Politics* 1:197-220.
McDill, Edward L. 1961. "Anomie, Authoritarianism, Prejudice, and Socioeconomic Status: An Attempt at Clarification." *Social Forces* 39:239-245.
McKenzie, Robert and Allan Silver. 1968. *Angels in Marble: Working Class Conservatives in Urban England*. London: Heineman.
Mead, Lawrence M. 1986. *Beyond Entitlement: The Social Obligations of Citizenship*. New York: Free Press.
Mény, Yves and Yves Surel. 2000. *Par le peuple, pour le peuple: Le populisme et les démocraties* [By the People, For the People: Populism and the Democracies] Paris: Fayard.
Middendorp, Cees P. 1978. *Progressiveness and Conservatism: The Fundamental Dimensions of Ideological Controversy and Their Relationship to Social Class*. Den Haag: Mouton.
Middendorp, Cees P. 1991. *Ideology in Dutch Politics: The Democratic System Reconsidered (1970-1985)*. Assen: Van Gorcum.

Middendorp, Cees P. and Jos D. Meloen. 1990. "The Authoritarianism of the Working Class Revisited." *European Journal of Political Research* 18:257-267.

Mitchell, Robert Edward. 1966. "Class-Linked Conflict between Two Dimensions of Liberalism-Conservatism." *Social Problems* 13:418-427.

Mouw, Ted and Michael E. Sobel. 2001. "Culture Wars and Opinion Polarization: The Case of Abortion." *American Journal of Sociology* 106:913-943.

Mudde, Cas. 2000. *The Ideology of the Extreme Right.* Manchester: Manchester University Press.

Murray, Charles. 1984. *Losing Ground: American Social Policy 1950-1980.* New York: Basic Books.

Niehof, Jacques. 1997. *Resources and Social Reproduction: The Effects of Cultural and Material Resources on Educational and Occupational Careers in Industrial Nations at the End of the Twentieth Century.* Groningen/Utrecht/Nijmegen: ICS.

Nieuwbeerta, Paul. 1995. *The Democratic Class Struggle in Twenty Countries, 1945-1990.* Amsterdam: Thesis Publishers.

Nieuwbeerta, Paul. 1996. "The Democratic Class Struggle in Postwar Societies: Class Voting in Twenty Countries, 1945-1990." *Acta Sociologica* 39:345-384.

Nieuwbeerta, Paul. 2001. "The Democratic Class Struggle in Postwar Societies: Traditional Class Voting in Twenty Countries, 1945-1990." Pp. 121-135 in *The Breakdown of Class Politics: A Debate on Post-Industrial Stratification*, edited by Terry Nichols Clark and Seymour Martin Lipset. Baltimore, MD: Johns Hopkins University Press.

Nieuwbeerta, Paul and Nan Dirk De Graaf. 1999. "Traditional Class Voting in Twenty Postwar Societies" Pp. 23-58 in *The End of Class Politics? Class Voting in Comparative Perspective*, edited by Geoffrey Evans. Oxford: Oxford University Press.

Nieuwbeerta, Paul and Harry Ganzeboom. 1996. *International Social Mobility and Politics File: Documentation of an Integrated Dataset of 113 National Surveys Held in 16 countries, 1956-1991 [Codebook].* Amsterdam: Steinmetz Archive.

Nieuwbeerta, Paul and Wout C. Ultee. 1999. "Class Voting in Western Industrialized Countries, 1945-1990: Systematizing and Testing Explanations." *European Journal of Political Research* 35:123-160.

O'Kane, James M. 1970. "Economic and Noneconomic Liberalism, Upward Mobility Potential, and Catholic Working Class Youth." *Social Forces* 40:499-506.

Olson, Daniel V.A. and Jackson W. Carroll. 1992. "Religiously Based Politics: Religious Elites and the Public." *Social Forces* 70:913-944.

Pakulski, Jan. 2001. "Class Paradigm and Politics." Pp. 137-161 in *The Breakdown of Class Politics: A Debate on Post-Industrial Stratification*, edited by Terry Nichols Clark and Seymour Martin Lipset. Baltimore, MD: Johns Hopkins University Press.

Pakulski, Jan and Malcolm Waters. 1996. *The Death of Class.* London: Sage.

Papadopoulos, Yannis. 2001. "El nacional populismo en Europa occidental: Un fenomeno ambivalente" [National Populism in Western Europe: An Ambiguous Phenomenon]. Pp. 65-105 in *Del populismo de los antiguos al populismo de los modernos* [On Old and Modern Populism], edited by Guy Hermet, Soledad Loaeza, and Jean-Francois Prud'homme. Mexico: El Colegio de México.

Pierson, Paul. 1994. *Dismantling the Welfare State? Reagan, Thatcher and the Politics of Retrenchment.* Cambridge: Cambridge University Press.

Poe, Edgar Allan. 1990 [1844]. "The Premature Burial." Pp. 308-315 in: *The Short Fiction of Edgar Allan Poe: An Annotated Edition.* Urbana/Chicago: University of Illinois Press.

Ransford, H. Edward. 1972. "Blue-Collar Anger: Reactions to Student and Black Protest." *American Sociological Review* 37:333-346.

Reid, Ivan. 1977. *Social Class Differences in Britain.* London: Open Books.
Rempel, Michael and Terry Nichols Clark. 1997. "Post-Industrial Politics: A Framework for Interpreting Citizen Politics Since the 1960s." Pp. 9-56 in *Citizen Politics in Post-Industrial Societies,* edited by Michael Rempel and Terry Nichols Clark. Boulder, CO: Westview Press.
Roberts, Alan H. and Milton Rokeach. 1956. "Anomie, Authoritarianism, and Prejudice: A Replication." *American Journal of Sociology* 61:355-358.
Robinson, Alan D. 1967. "Class Voting in New Zealand: A Comment on Alford's Comparison of Class Voting in the Anglo-American Political Systems." Pp. 95-114 in *Party Systems and Voter Alignments: Cross-National Perspectives,* edited by Seymour Martin Lipset and Stein Rokkan. New York: Free Press.
Rose, Richard and Ian McAllister. 1986. *Voters Begin to Choose: From Closed-Class to Open Elections in Britain.* London: Sage.
Roszak, Theodore. 1969. *The Making of a Counter Culture: Reflections on the Technocratic Society and Its Youthful Opposition.* New York: Doubleday.
Sanders, David. 1999. "The Impact of Left-Right Ideology." Pp. 181-206 in *Critical Elections,* edited by Geoffrey Evans and Pippa Norris. London: Sage.
Sapiro, Virginia, Steven J. Rosenstone, and the National Election Studies. 2002. *American National Election Studies Cumulative Data File, 1948-2000 [Computer file], 11th ICPSR version.* University of Michigan, Center for Political Studies [producer]/ Interuniversity Consortium for Political and Social Research [distributor], Ann Arbor.
Scheepers, Peer, Rob Eisinga, and Leo Van Snippenburg. 1992. "Working-Class Authoritarianism: Evaluation of a Research Tradition and an Empirical Test." *Netherlands' Journal of Social Sciences* 28:103-126.
Schippers, Joop. 1995. "Pay Differences Between Men and Women in the European Labour Market." Pp. 31-52 in *Women and the European Labour Markets,* edited by Anneke Van Doorne-Huiskes, Jacques Van Hoof, and Ellie Roelofs. London: Paul Chapman.
Simmons, Solon. 2004. "What's the Big Idea? The Continuing Relevance of the Democratic Class Struggle." Paper presented at the Annual Meeting of the *American Sociological Association.* San Francisco, August 13-16 2006.
Slack, Paul. 1988. *Poverty and Policy in Tudor and Stuart England.* London/New York: Longman.
Srole, Leo. 1956. "Social Integration and Certain Corrolaries: An Exploratory Study". *American Sociological Review* 21:709-716.
Steel, Brent S., Rebecca L. Warner, Nicholas P. Lovrich, and John C. Pierce. 1992. "The Inglehart-Flanagan Debate over Postmaterialist Values: Some Evidence From a Canadian-American Case Study." *Political Psychology* 13:61-77.
Stehr, Nico. 1994. *Knowledge Societies.* London: Sage
Steijn, Bram and Dick Houtman. 1998. "Proletarianization of the Dutch Middle Class: Fact or Fiction?" Pp. 73-91 in *Economic Restructuring and the Growing Uncertainty of the Middle Class,* edited by Bram Steijn, Jan Berting and Mart-Jan De Jong. Boston: Kluwer.
Stonecash, Jeffrey. M. 2000. *Class and Party in American Politics.* Boulder, CO: Westview Press.
Svallfors, Stefan. 1999. "Political Trust and Attitudes towards Redistribution: A Comparison of Sweden and Norway." *European Societies* 1:241-268.
Swyngedouw, Marc. 1994. "De opkomst en doorbraak van Agalev en Vlaams Blok in de jaren tachtig en negentig" [The Rise and Success of Agalev and Vlaams Blok in the Eighties and Nineties]. *Acta Politica* 29:453-476.
Swyngedouw, Marc. 1998 "The Extreme Right in Belgium: Of a Non-Existing Front National and an Omnipresent Vlaams Blok." Pp. 59-76 in *The Politics of the Right:*

Neo-Populist Parties and Movements in Established Democracies, edited by Hans-Georg Betz and Stefan Immerfall. London: Macmillan.
Taggart, Paul. 2002. "Populism and the Pathology of Representative Politics." Pp. 62-80 in *Democracies and the Populist Challenge*, edited by Yves Mény and Yves Surel. Houndmills: Palgrave.
Van de Werfhorst, Herman G. and Nan Dirk De Graaf. 2004. "The Sources of Political Orientations in Post-Industrial Society: Social Class and Education Revisited." *British Journal of Sociology* 55:211-236.
Van Oorschot, Wim 1998. "Deservingness and Conditionality of Solidarity." *Sociale Wetenschappen* 41:54-78.
Van Parijs, Phillippe (Ed.). 1992. *Arguing for Basic Income: Ethical Foundations for a Radical Reform.* London: Verso.
Veugelers, John W.P. 2000. "Right-Wing Extremism in Contemporary France: A 'Silent Counterrevolution'?" *Sociological Quarterly* 41:19-40.
Weakliem, David L. 2001. "Social Class and Voting: The Case Against Decline." Pp. 197-224 in *The Breakdown of Class Politics: A Debate on Post-Industrial Stratification*, edited by Terry Nichols Clark and Seymour Martin Lipset. Baltimore, MD: Johns Hopkins University Press.
Weakliem, David L. and Anthony F. Heath. 1994. "Rational Choice and Class Voting." *Rationality and Society* 6:243-271.
Weakliem, David L. and Anthony Heath. 1999a. "The Secret Life of Class Voting: Britain, France and the United States Since the 1930s." Pp. 97-136 in *The End of Class Politics? Class Voting in Comparative Context*, edited by Geoffrey Evans. Oxford: Oxford University Press.
Weakliem, David L. and Anthony Heath. 1999b. "Resolving Disputes about Class Voting in Britain and the United States: Definitions, Models, and Data." Pp. 281-307 in *The End of Class Politics? Class Voting in Comparative Context*, edited by Geoffrey Evans. Oxford: Oxford University Press.
Weber, Max. 1978 [1921]. *Economy and Society (Volume I).* Berkeley/Los Angeles: University of California Press.
Wilensky, Harold L. 1975. *The Welfare State and Equality: Structural and Ideological Roots of Public Expenditures*. Berkeley: University of California Press.
Wiles, Peter. 1969. "A Syndrome, Not a Doctrine: Some Elementary Theses on Populism." Pp. 166-179 in *Populism: Its Meanings and National Caracteristics*, edited by Ghita Ionescu and Ernest Gellner. London: Weidenfeld and Nicolson.
Wilson, Bryan. 1982. *Religion in Sociological Perspective*. Oxford: Oxford University Press.
Wright, Erik Olin. 1979. *Class Structure and Income Determination.* New York: Academic Press.
Wright, Erik Olin. 1985. *Classes.* London: Verso.
Zijderveld, Anton C. 1970. *The Abstract Society: A Cultural Analysis of Our Time.* Garden City: Doubleday.
Zijderveld, Anton C. 1999. *The Waning of the Welfare State: The End of Comprehensive State Succor.* New Brunswick/NJ: Transaction.
Zijderveld, Anton C. 2000. *The Institutional Imperative: The Interface of Institutions and Networks.* Amsterdam: Amsterdam University Press.
Zweig, Ferdynand. 1961. *The Worker in an Affluent Society: Family Life and Industry.* London: Heinemann.

About the Authors

Peter Achterberg (Dordrecht, the Netherlands, 1977) completed his Ph.D. thesis *Considering Cultural Conflict* at Erasmus University's Department of Sociology in 2006 and now holds a postdoctoral position at the same department, studying problems of solidarity and popular support for state-supported social care arrangements. In addition to Dutch journals, his articles have been published by international journals such as *European Journal of Political Research* and *International Sociology*.

Anton Derks (Geel, Belgium, 1969) is a researcher at the Flemish Ministry of Education and a guest professor at the Free University Brussels, Belgium, teaching a course on modernization. His main research areas are the sociology of culture and political sociology, with his most recent work examining public support for the welfare state in relation to social class, ideology and voting behavior. Since the completion of his Ph.D. thesis, *Individualisme zonder verhaal* [Individualism without a Cause] in 2000, he has co-authored two books in Dutch and—in addition to other publications in Dutch—has also written book chapters in English and articles in *Ethical Perspectives*, *Res Publica*, *European Journal of Political Research*, and *World Political Science Review*.

Dick Houtman (Utrecht, the Netherlands, 1963) is Professor of.Sociology of Culture at Erasmus University and a member of the Amsterdam School for Social science Research (ASSR). Political and religious ramifications of cultural change in late modernity constitute his principal research interest. His latest book, *Class and Politics in Contemporary Social Science*, has been published by Aldine de Gruyter in 2003 and his articles have appeared in journals such as *Social Justice Research*, *Journal for the Scientific Study of Religion*, *European Journal of Political Research*, *British Journal of Criminology*, and *Journal of Contemporary Religion*.

Jeroen van der Waal (Sliedrecht, the Netherlands, 1974) is a Ph.D. student at Erasmus University's Department of Sociology since 2005, studying the consequences of globalization for urban inequality in the western world. Two international articles on culture and politics, based on his BA and MA theses, have appeared in *Politics & Society* (with Peter Achterberg and Dick Houtman) and *International Political Science Review* (with Willem de Koster) in 2007.

rightist party voting, 16, 79-88
"unnatural voting," 16, 19, 23-29, 37

welfare state, 2, 4-5, 9-11, 91-93, 114
workfare, 94, 96

working class,
    economic position, 2
    leftist working class, 1
    rightist working class, 1
    voting patterns, 2-4

Index

Alford, Robert R., 8, 37
Alford Index, 9
American Election Studies, 38, 45
authoritarianism, 17-19, 20-21, 105 (see also libertarianism)

Belgium, 106-108
Bell, Daniel, 55
Bourdieu, Pierre, 18

capitalism, 10
class
    distribution, 21-25, 41
    polarization, 61-66
    struggle, 55
    theory of politics, 1-4, 15, 17, 40, 47-51, 91-92, 119-121
culture, 21, 98

Dittrich, Boris, 55

economic egalitarianism/conservatism, 20
economy,
    class-based, 16, 20
    populism, 109-115
education, 21, 77-78
Engels, Friedrich, 3

"false consciousness," 115
Fukuyama, Francis, 55

Horowitz, Irving L., 105

income, 20, 71, 76, 94
individual liberties, 6
Inglehart, Ronald, 5, 18, 39-40, 58, 61
issue salience, 40-42, 45, 51, 56-61, 71, 124-125

Kautsky, Karl, 3

Lenin, Vladimir, 3
libertarianism, 18-19, 20-21, 39, 94-95, 115 (see also libertarianism)
Lipset, Seymour Martin, 38, 105

Marx, Karl,
    capitalism, 10
    letters from Engels, 3
    theory of Universal Suffrage, 2
modernity, 122-124

Netherlands, 29-34, 93-94
Nieuwbeerta, Paul, 1, 2, 4, 56, 71, 73, 75-76

Party Manifesto Data, 56
political culture, 38, 68-69
populism, 106-107
postmaterialism, 5-6, 17-18, 39, 44, 61

Reid, Ivan, 16

salaried employment, 20
Second Reform Bill, 2
Stonecash, Jeffrey M., 74

thesis of *embourgeoisement*, 3-4, 9-11

unemployment, 94, 101
United States,
    elections, 38, 45, 47-51

van der Waal, Jeroen, 71-88
Verelendung, 3
voting,
    behavior, 21, 37, 45, 77-78
    class voting, 6-8, 15, 17, 43-44, 71-72, 74
    cultural voting, 6-8, 72-73
    measuring voting patterns, 8, 15
    leftist party voting, 16-17, 72-73